G000067012

Shooting and Stalking

Shooting and Stalking

A Basic Guide

Edited by Charles Coles

Stanley Paul
London Melbourne Sydney Auckland Johannesburg

Stanley Paul & Co. Ltd

An imprint of Century Hutchinson Ltd
Brookmount House, 62–65 Chandos Place, Covent Garden,
London WC2N 4NW

Hutchinson Publishing Group (Australia) Pty Ltd
16–22 Church Street, Hawthorn, Melbourne, Victoria 3122

Hutchinson Group (NZ) Ltd
32–34 View Road, PO Box 40-086, Glenfield, Auckland 10

Hutchinson Group (SA) Pty Ltd
PO Box 337, Bergvlei 2012, South Africa

First published 1983
Reprinted 1985
© Fédération des Associations de Chasseurs Européens (FACE)
UK 1983

Set in Monophoto Bembo

Printed in Great Britain by Balding + Mansell Limited,
Wisbech, Cambridgeshire
and bound by Anchor Brendon Ltd,
Tiptree, Essex
ISBN 0 09 153530 1

Frontispiece: *Pheasant shooting in the
Yorkshire Dales on a winter's day*

Contents

Foreword

by Lord Porchester, KBE, DL, Chairman of the Standing Conference on
Countryside Sports

While there are a great number of interesting treatises on shooting and
some excellent technical publications on game management, up till now
there has not been a single wide-ranging work dealing with all the basic
essentials that a sportsman should know. Here, for the first time, we have
something similar to a Highway Code for everyone who goes out in the
field with shotgun or rifle.

Two or three decades ago most sportsmen had a country background.
At an early age father, elder brother or gamekeeper would initiate the
young shot – often quite strictly – into the ways of the true sportsman.
This tutelage usually went far beyond just shooting with care and
consideration: it provided a broad understanding of the countryside and
the problems of the farmer, the forester and the people who lived and
worked on the land. Today, many more of our sportsmen come from the
towns and while the urban-based shot may be forgiven for not
recognizing a Brimstone butterfly or even knowing wheat from barley,
he should not begin to use a sporting weapon until he has acquired a
sensible understanding of the sport: the laws governing shooting, a
knowledge of which species are protected, how to behave correctly in the
field and something of the gamekeeper's skills.

In my opinion this guide – in addition to helping the less experienced
shot – also has a place on the bookshelves of the sportsman who has been
shooting all his life.

Introduction

Over a hundred and fifty years ago the famous Col. Peter Hawker wrote his *Instructions to Young Shooters*. The book was criticized by a friend as being 'dictatorial and egotistical' and certainly the sporting Colonel was keener on killing than on conservation; but it was, and still is, a classic. It is a very comprehensive treatise and, in addition to what it said about shooting in general, the game laws of the day, cleaning guns and so on, it is very entertaining – sometimes unintentionally. The reader is instructed in how to dress 'so as always to appear like a gentleman', and in the medical section special tinctures of bark are recommended 'as an effective stimulus to brace the nerves of a bad shot'!

In this present book we have come down to earth. The concept of producing an up-to-date version of Col. Hawker's *Instructions* was the idea of a number of organizations concerned with shooting and stalking. They included the British Association for Shooting and Conservation, the British Deer Society, the British Field Sports Society, the Game Conservancy and the St Hubert Club.

Today's sportsman has to acquire his knowledge and build up his experience more quickly than he did a generation ago, as most young people start shooting at a later age and many take it up in middle age. The well-known poem 'A Father's Advice' (quoted on page 47) was written by a father for his son on reaching the age of thirteen. Today, in our increasingly urban surroundings and because the law is more restrictive, few are able to start handling guns so young.

The purpose of this book is to serve the less experienced sportsman as a basic guide which will give him the advice and essential knowledge to enable him to shoot safely and with confidence. It is also hoped that the book will act as an introduction to game management, the science or craft concerned with the survival of our quarry species and other forms of wildlife.

Royalties will be donated to FACE (UK) (Fédération des Associations de Chasseurs de la CEE). FACE is the body that serves as the official British field-sports representation at the EEC in Brussels; it is recognized by the Council of Europe. Amongst other things it acts as a watchdog on EEC legislative activities on behalf of all UK sportsmen and endeavours to ensure that decisions taken in Brussels are based on accurate facts rather than on opinions which may be politically motivated. FACE is also concerned with general wildlife conservation and provides a forum for information and ideas from colleagues in other EEC countries. It is engaged in encouraging research into game, wildfowl and wildlife on an international basis.

Many of the authors, artists and photographers who have contributed to this book have charged either no fee for their work or only a nominal sum. To them we owe our most grateful thanks.

C.L. COLES

I

Shooting and Conservation

The purpose of this book is to explain the main points with which a sportsman should be familiar when using shotgun and rifle in the field.

It discusses the essential game laws and other relevant legislation, the safe handling of weapons and the behaviour expected of a shooter by fellow sportsmen. It also attempts to outline something of the skilled management required to safeguard the welfare of game in a countryside which is shrinking every year and which grows increasingly hostile to many wildlife species. This is to some extent due to intensive farming, the destruction of hedgerows and other cover, and the misuse of chemical sprays such as pesticides. The keen shooting farmer strives to keep all this in balance. The considerate shooter is a good conservationist and is careful to put back more than he takes out. This relationship of the hunter to his quarry is at the heart of good shooting and stalking.

We believe it is essential for every 'hunter' – to use the continental and American expression – to know something about his quarry, as well as the other wildlife species that he is likely to meet when out shooting. The skills required to manage game and wildfowl habitat and produce a satisfactory harvest of partridge, grouse, pheasant, wild duck – or whatever may be appropriate to the local conditions – are as necessary and worthwhile as, and perhaps even more demanding than, the mere ability to be a good shot. It is also useful for a shooting man to collect and interpret records of the game he shoots. This includes being able to distinguish young birds from old, cocks from hens, and so on. Acquiring this knowledge should be part of a young shot's apprenticeship.

A certain amount of repetition has been intended and we hope readers will not find it too frustrating. Our reason for this – often on the subject of safety or ethics – is the possibility of a reader consulting one section in isolation, without having previously studied an earlier relevant one.

There is insufficient room here to deal with any subject in depth, but the authors hope that this book will stimulate further study. No written work, however, can take the place of practical knowledge acquired in the field – of time spent with experienced shots, gamekeepers, stalkers and others. Nevertheless, we believe that this book will contribute towards the reader becoming a safe, responsible shot, whose company will be enjoyed by others wherever he goes.

2

The Different Types of Shooting

Sport with shotgun or rifle comes in many forms and can vary from decoying woodpigeons in a hide to shooting driven grouse on a well managed moor. It may surprise some to hear that many sportsmen get as much satisfaction, excitement and as many difficult shots when out pigeon shooting as they do on a grouse moor.

The surroundings of a grouse moor, the colours and the majesty of the purple hills, the quality of the picnic, perhaps the presence of a pony-man and other such trappings, are possibly unique. One can therefore understand that the pigeon shooter may momentarily feel envious of the Guns on the moor, when sitting cramped-up in a leafy hide cursing the midges, with a packet of ham sandwiches and a bottle of beer. Perhaps one should not compare the two? For there is something about pigeon shooting that in its own way is very special. As well as being a good shot, one also has to be an expert in fieldcraft and this provides an added satisfaction. Ferreting, wildfowling or stalking the red stags are all different and each has its own devotees.

Driving and Walking-Up

Shooting with a shotgun can broadly be divided into two kinds. The first consists of *walking-up* the quarry through farm crops or woodland, on moorland or marsh. The second involves having the birds *driven* towards a line of Guns, usually concealed behind a hedge or belt of trees, or half-hidden in a grouse butt. Some birds are more wary than others: if, for example, a pheasant is committed to a certain flight line and making resolutely for a favourite roosting wood or food crop, the line of Guns can usually stand out in the open and the birds will generally continue to fly more or less straight on. On seeing the Guns they may twist in the air or gain height, which helps to provide a more testing shot. As the season progresses, however, pheasants become more experienced and suspicious and, on sighting the Guns, will often turn back or slip out at the side of the covert. In an effort to outwit these evasion tactics a shoot manager will try to position a flank or walking Gun in a strategic place, or drive the birds in a different direction if this is feasible.

Driven game tends to provide a more formal day and is invariably much more expensive because the host has to supply a team of beaters. The birds are usually travelling faster than those that are walked-up and theoretically should provide more spectacular shooting, though this is not always the case.

A driven covey of grouse approach the butt and one is shot. The butt is a good, sturdy construction of stones, topped with turf and heather

Walking up game with spaniels. (Photograph kindly donated by John Marchington)

On some smaller shoots where driven birds are appreciated, the Guns often split into two groups and take it in turns to stand in the line at the 'receiving end', and for the following beat to undertake the driving. Care must be taken by those walking *not* to shoot birds going forward, but only birds going out at the side or passing behind: in other words, the walking Guns must not spoil the sport for the standing Guns.

On such days it will naturally improve the efficiency of the driving if a few extra beaters can be employed, so as to stretch the line across the field or the woodland without leaving too many gaps. In this case the line is usually spaced out so that at least one beater is between each Gun. Two beaters between each Gun are even better. Wives, responsible children and volunteers who enjoy the exercise and will almost certainly be given a pheasant to take home, can often be persuaded to make up part of the team, in addition to the paid hands.

Such walk-and-stand shooting is not always possible or it may not be what the organizer wants to do. Many small shoots are happy to go after walked-up game all day; though they will certainly have some flank Guns well forward to cut off birds that would otherwise rise out of shot, far ahead of the line. Walking-up is not as simple as it sounds: the direction and strength of the wind, for example, have to be taken into consideration when deciding which way to go through a piece of cover.

It is clearly very unsporting to fire at a pheasant rising out of a crop just a few yards ahead of the Gun, so as to kill it before your neighbour does. Such a shot will be too easy; the bird will be filled with pellets and unsuitable for the table. Judgement of range is important and comes with experience. The greedy, trigger-happy guest is rarely asked a second time.

On the other hand one can be too clever and wait too long while the bird is flying away, in which case the quarry may be taken at too great a distance, be wounded in the back and fly on. Should this happen it is essential to carry out a thorough search for the bird; no shooting party should ever set out without sufficient experienced gundogs. This subject is explained more fully in chapter five, 'Good Sportsmanship and Behaviour in the Field'.

The smaller shoot, where walking-up is mostly the order of the day, is often called a 'rough shoot'. Normally this means that the acreage may be fairly modest, though some rough shoots can extend over miles of marsh or marginal ground; and it is unlikely that a fulltime keeper will be

Three rough shooters and their dogs. (Photograph kindly donated by John Marchington)

employed. The feeding, trapping, perhaps some rearing, and the game management in general, is likely to be undertaken by the owner himself or a part-time keeper; or, if it is a syndicate, by members of the shoot in their spare time. Unfortunately, there are some rough shoots where the owner or the lessee of the ground does nothing at all in the way of management or re-stocking.

There may, of course, be one or two variations regarding what is an accepted practice on a particular shoot, and it is essential to find this out at the start of the day. For instance, on a formal day, shotguns are always unloaded between drives and no shooting then takes place until the next drive. Should a bird fly over while the picking-up is still in progress or while the Guns are walking back to the vehicles, no shot should be taken. The head keeper or head beater should always clearly indicate when a drive is over, by calling out, blowing a whistle or sounding a horn.

On a less formal day, where shots are likely to be few and far between, your host may explain that he is not going to have any 'set pieces' during the day, but intends to range across the countryside almost without a break. On such an occasion, if the Guns stop for any reason and a safe shot presents itself, a guest would be expected *not* to miss the opportunity of adding to the bag. But care is required: it is rather embarrassing if three people all fire together!

Whether invited to a 'rough shoot' or a more formal shoot, the standard of behaviour and sportsmanship expected is exactly the same.

Flighting

Some quarry, such as wildfowl, woodpigeons, even carrion crows, can be 'flighted'; the Gun stations himself where he is likely to intercept the birds on a regular or anticipated passage between feeding and roosting grounds, and vice versa. In this case the sportsman must have a good local knowledge of the birds' habits and flight-lines. Previous reconnaissance, a knowledge of the disposition of the feeding grounds, weather conditions and so on, are usually essential.

More details about flighting will be found in the relevant chapters.

Shooting over Dogs

Game can also be shot over pointers and setters – and occasionally other breeds – which find their quarry by scent and then 'freeze', indicating to the handler that hidden in some cover a few feet away there is a pheasant, a covey of grouse or whatever it may be.

At a command from the handler the dog will flush the quarry and the Gun take his shot. Shooting over dogs is a rather specialized pursuit but it is one of the more attractive sports in that it relies on the skilled partnership of a man and his dog. Working spaniels in cover is also another form of partnership that demands patience in training and handling.

Rifle Shooting and Stalking

Different types of stalking and other forms of rifle shooting are dealt with in later chapters of this book.

3
Taking Up Shooting – Where Can I Shoot?

Although this is dealt with in chapter four, 'The Law and Shooting', some general introductory remarks may be helpful at this stage.

In Great Britain, game belongs to the owner of the land, just like his cattle and the farm crops that he grows. They are, in simple language, his private property, at least while they are on his land. This applies also to all quarry species which can be shot by sportsmen, but are not defined as 'game' by law: rabbit and woodpigeon, for example, would come into this category. The owner can shoot those species permitted by law; he can invite friends to shoot or he can let the shooting rights for money, just as he can let his grazing. There are various other arrangements into which he can enter.

Our laws, therefore, mean that a sportsman cannot – without permission from the holder of the sporting rights – walk over somebody else's land or enter somebody else's wood and use his gun, even at a pest like a carrion crow.

If one does not own any suitable land for shooting it is necessary to join a club or syndicate or to find out from local farmers whether any shooting is legitimately available.

Wildfowling around the coast comes into another category.

4

The Law and Shooting

1   In England and Wales it is only legal to shoot on:

    i One's own land over which the sporting rights are retained, or

    ii Land with the permission of the landowner who has retained the sporting rights, or

    iii Land with the permission of the occupier who holds the sporting rights, or

    iv Land with the permission of the holder of the sporting rights but who neither owns nor occupies the land, or

    v One's own land where the sporting rights are let and one is in occupation provided only ground game (hares and rabbits) are shot.

    The only exception to the foregoing is where, in certain areas and circumstances, the public may be allowed to shoot on the foreshore. The public has no general right of shooting or otherwise taking quarry species on the foreshore although, where the Crown is the owner, it will probably acquiesce in the exercise of a right to shoot when this causes no mischief or injury. The foreshore is defined as: 'The land between high and low-water mark, being limited landwards to the median line of the high tide between spring and neap tides' (England and Wales).

2   In Scotland the situation is different. Although the landowner has the absolute right to the deer and game, the occupier has the right to kill wild animals and birds – other than deer or game – unless the landlord has expressly reserved that right. Occupiers of agricultural land and enclosed woodlands have the right to kill hares and rabbits

on their land though these rights are restricted on open moorlands or unenclosed lands. There is a further restriction to the effect that such occupiers may not kill hares and rabbits by the use of firearms, though they may take or kill by other means, between 1 April and 1 July in any year. The public has a right to shoot on the foreshore, this area being defined as: 'The land between the high and low-water mark of ordinary spring tides' (Scotland).

3   It is an offence to discharge a firearm within 50ft(15m)[1] of the centre of a public highway if by so doing a user of the highway is obstructed or endangered in any way.

4   Entry on land without permission in pursuit of game constitutes the offence of poaching and, if in pursuit of other wild animals or birds with a firearm, may constitute the offence of armed trespass.

5   Working dogs are not required to wear a collar bearing the name and address of the owner while they are working.[2] Although it is an offence for a dog to be at large (that is, not on a lead or otherwise under close control) in a field or enclosure in which there are sheep, an exception is made in the case of a working gundog. The meaning of 'close control' is not defined but the implications should generally be clear.

Firearms

6   A firearm is defined as: 'A lethal barrelled weapon of any description from which any shot, bullet or other missile can be discharged.' There are two main types of firearm used for shooting in the field in this country.

7   *Rifles*[3] These are used for shooting mammals such as deer, hares, rabbits, squirrels, etc. To own or use a rifle, a Firearm Certificate is required to cover each rifle and the ammunition for it. The certificate is granted by the police who are entitled to require 'a good reason' for the issue on payment of the appropriate fee.

1. The authors have thought it expedient to give measurements in both imperial and metric, except where one or the other is in common use such as in ballistic tables.

2. In spite of what the Law says regarding the freedom of gundogs *not* to wear a collar whilst out working, owners of dogs should take obvious precautions, which may involve collar and lead, when they are on, or near, roads – busy or otherwise.

3. See also chapter twenty-three, 'Firearms for Deer'.

8 *Shotguns* These are used for shooting birds of all descriptions and also for smaller mammals such as hares, rabbits, squirrels, etc. To own and use a shotgun, a Shotgun Certificate is usually required. The certificate is issued by the police on payment of the appropriate fee. The certificate entitles the owner to possess any number of unspecified shotguns and no certificate is required to acquire or possess shotgun ammunition. A person who has been in this country for not more than thirty days in all, in the preceding twelve months, does not require a Shotgun Certificate.

9 *Certificates* In the case of both certificates the police require to satisfy themselves that the applicant is not likely to be a danger to the public safety or the peace and, in addition, in the case of a Firearm Certificate, is not of intemperate habits or unsound mind or for any other reason unfitted to be entrusted with such a firearm. Certificates continue in force for three years after which they may be renewed for further periods of three years. It is always advisable to carry the appropriate certificate when carrying or using a firearm or shotgun to produce if required to do so by a police officer.

10 *Young Persons* Special provisions apply to the possession and use of firearms in the field by young persons of various ages.

   i *Under Fourteen* May only be in possession of firearms, or ammunition, while under instruction by a certificate holder and for sporting purposes only.

   ii *Under Fifteen* May only have an assembled shotgun while under supervision of a person of, or over, the age of twenty-one or in a cover so that it cannot be fired.

   iii *Under Seventeen* May not purchase or hire any firearm or ammunition.

    It is also an offence to sell, or let on hire, any firearm/ammunition/shotgun (as appropriate) to the persons in the above categories. It is also an offence for persons in category (i) to be in possession of any air weapon except under the circumstances as specified.

11 *Illegal Weapons and Ammunition* The following weapons and ammunition may not be used to kill wild animals or birds.

   i *Firearms* Automatic or semi-automatic weapons[1], the magazines of which are capable of holding more than two rounds; any

---

1. See also chapter eight, 'Sporting Guns and Cartridges,' for more details.

shotgun with a barrel less than 24ins(610mm) in length. In the case of birds any shotgun which has an internal diameter at the muzzle of more than $1\frac{3}{4}$ins(44mm).

ii *Others* Bows or cross-bows.

iii *Ammunition* Cartridges containing less than five shot any of which exceeds 0.36ins(9mm) in diameter.

12   *Public Places* It is an offence if, without lawful authority or reasonable excuse, a person has with him in a public place a loaded shotgun or a rifle (whether loaded or not), together with ammunition suitable for use in that rifle. It is also an offence for any person who, while he has a firearm with him, enters, or is on, any land or in any building or part of the building as a trespasser and without lawful excuse. If at any time it is found necessary to carry a firearm in a public place it should be carried in a securely fastened slip or case.

Wild Animals

13   *Ownership* Wild animals, and these include any game not in captivity, cannot be stolen. The holder of the sporting rights of the land on which they are present has the exclusive right to take possession of them, but they do not become his property until he has actually taken them into his physical possession. Once they have been killed or otherwise taken into possession they become the property of the holder of the sporting rights, no matter who has killed or taken them.

14   *Quarry Species* For convenience these are classified in three categories:

   i *Game* These are defined variously in different statutes but generally include those birds or animals listed under 1 on page 28, and require anyone who takes or kills any of them to be in possession of a licence to do so.

   ii *Wildfowl and Other Species* These, mainly consisting of wildfowl and some waders, are listed under 2 (page 28); no licence is required to take or kill them.

   iii *Vermin* Birds are listed under 3 (page 29)and some mammals which may be encountered on shooting days are also listed there; no licence is required to kill or take them.

15   *Protected Species*

   i *Birds* All birds in this country, other than those listed on pages

28 and 29, are fully protected at all times of the year and these include all species of hawks and owls. Penalties for killing or attempting to kill protected birds are severe and in the case of specially protected species are extremely severe.

ii *Mammals* On page 29, number 4 lists certain mammals to which a degree of protection is afforded; some of these may be encountered on shooting days.

16   *Close Seasons, Days and Times*

i *Close Seasons* Where these exist they are shown in lists 1 and 2 and the dates are inclusive in every case. There are no close seasons for species listed in 3 and 4, Part 2.

ii *Days* Species shown in list 1 may not be shot on a Sunday or Christmas Day. In Scotland and in certain local-authority areas in England and Wales no shooting of any wild bird or animal is permitted on a Sunday or Christmas Day.

iii *Times* It is an offence to shoot any of the species shown in list 1 at night. However, hares (list 1) and rabbits (list 3, Part 2) may be shot at night but only by those persons permitted to do so under the Ground Game Act 1880 in England and Wales and under the Agriculture (Scotland) Act 1948 in Scotland. Both these Acts have been recently amended by Schedule 7 of the Wildlife & Countryside Act 1981.

Night is defined as: 'The period of the first hour after sunset until the first hour before sunrise, local time'.

Species shown in lists 2 and 3 may be shot at night but there are restrictions on the use of artificial light and similar aids in respect of the species shown in lists 2 and 3, Part 1.

17   *Illegal Methods*

i *Decoys* It is an offence to use as a decoy, for the purpose of killing any wild bird or mammal, any sound recording or any live bird or mammal which is tethered or secured by means of braces or other similar appliances, or which is blind, maimed or injured.

ii *Mechanically Propelled Vehicles* It is an offence to use any mechanically propelled vehicles – including aircraft, hovercraft and boat – in immediate pursuit of any wild bird or mammal for the purpose of killing or taking it and also, in the case of a mammal, for driving it.

iii *Others* It is an offence to use any form of artificial lighting, mirror, or any device for dazzling, illuminating a target for night shooting, for killing or taking any wild bird or any mammal shown in list 4, page 29.

Licences

18   Licences to kill game or to deal in game are available at most post offices on payment of the appropriate fee.

i *To Kill Game* The following categories are available:
   a. Annual expiring 31 July   £6
   b. Annual gamekeeper's expiring 31 July   £4
   c. Period 1 August to 31 October   £4
   d. Period 1 November to 31 July   £4
   e. Any period of fourteen days   £2

ii A gamekeeper's licence is transferable on application to the issuing authority; such a licence is only valid for use upon the land on which the holder is employed as a gamekeeper.

iii It is important to know that the licences in categories 18i.c. and d. cannot be obtained before 1 August and 1 November respectively.

iv *To Deal in Game* No person unless he is a licensed game dealer may sell game to, or buy game from, any other person unless that person is a licensed game dealer. A licensed dealer may only buy game from the holder of an annual licence to kill game or from another licensed game dealer.

v In England and Wales, in addition to the licence obtained from the post office to deal in game valid for one year at a cost of £4, an excise licence valid for one year and costing 25p must be obtained from the local authority by any person dealing in game.

vi In Scotland two licences are required and application should be made to the District Council; one is a game dealer's licence costing £4 and the other is a licence from a Justice of the Peace costing 80p.

1 Close Seasons for Gamebirds, Woodcock and Snipe

Blackgame	11 December to 19 August
Grouse	11 December to 11 August
Partridge	2 February to 31 August
Pheasant	2 February to 30 September
Ptarmigan	11 December to 11 August
Snipe, Common[1]	1 February to 11 August
Woodcock[1]	1 February to 30 September (England & Wales)
	1 February to 31 August (Scotland)
Hare	There is no close season for hares but the sale, offer or exposure for sale commencing with 1 March and ending with 31 July in any year, except in the case of foreign hares imported into the United Kingdom, is an offence.

Both days in this Appendix are inclusive, in every case.

1. Although not 'game' within the meaning of the Game Act 1831 nevertheless a game licence is required to take or kill them.

2 Close Seasons for Wildfowl and Other Species

Capercaillie	1 February to 30 September
Coot	
Moorhen	1 February to 31 August
Plover, Golden	

Wild Duck and Geese

Duck, Tufted	
Gadwall	
Goldeneye	
Goose, Canada	In or over any area below high-water
Goose, Greylag	mark of ordinary spring tides, the period
Goose, Pink-footed	in any year commencing with
Goose, White-fronted	21 February and ending with 31 August.
(in England and Wales only)	
Mallard	In any other area the period in any year
Pintail	commencing with 1 February and ending
Pochard	with 31 August.
Shoveler	
Teal	
Wigeon	

Both days in this Appendix are inclusive, in every case.

3 Vermin

Part 1

Birds

Crow
Dove, Collared
Gull, Great Black-backed
Gull, Lesser Black-backed
Gull, Herring
Jackdaw
Jay
Magpie
Pigeon, Feral
Rook
Sparrow, House
Starling
Woodpigeon

Part 2

Mammals

Cat, Feral
Coypu
Fox
Mink
Rabbit
Rat, Brown
Squirrel, Grey
Stoat
Weasel

There is no close season for any of the birds or mammals listed under 'Vermin'.

4 Protected Wild Animals

Part 1

At All Times

Otter, Common
Squirrel, Red

Part 2

**May Not be Taken
or Killed by Certain Methods**

Badger
Cat, Wild
Hedgehog
Marten, Pine
Polecat

5

Good Sportsmanship and Behaviour in the Field[1]

The rules of behaviour in the shooting field have been developed over the last two centuries. Moral, legal, practical, financial, historical, commercial, linguistic and safety aspects have been gradually incorporated, polished and perfected. They may now seem to be an odd assortment but they are a good one – ignored by the would-be sportsman at his peril.

The sport of shooting imposes certain obligations and, regardless of whether the day is given up to formal driven game, walking-up, rough shooting or wildfowling, these obligations vary only in degree.

The main enjoyment of shooting lies in pitting the hunter's skill against a demanding quarry: not simply killing it. The ethics of the sport also insist that the quarry should not suffer unnecessarily. An instant death by shooting – if it can be achieved – is better than the laws of nature usually allow.

Apart from taking heed of the laws which dictate what can be shot and when, a Gun must endeavour to be a naturalist, a marksman and a gentleman in the true sense of the word. The first implies recognition and knowledge of the quarry, as well as an appreciation of the role of field sports in conservation; the second the skill to shoot; and the third how to behave while doing so.

Without shooting – and the management of wildlife and habitat that complements it – many quarry species would not exist today. Others that do still exist would be uncommon or rare. The law, with its close seasons originally requested by sportsmen, provides protection from over-exploitation, and the game management provides the framework within

1. For the specialized sport of wildfowling see chapter fourteen, 'Wildfowling Today'.

which that protection can work. In practical terms this means maintaining a suitable wildlife habitat and other conditions for survival. The quarry is encouraged and the surplus is shot, leaving a strong nucleus to breed the following season.

Where game species thrive, so do other forms of wildlife. The benefits of shooting to conservation in general are incalculable, particularly in areas where farming pressures are severe.

To some people shooting a large bag, however it may be achieved, is proof of expertise of a sort. To the true sportsman one really difficult shot, with the bird killed stone dead, can give more satisfaction than any number of less testing ones. It is the difference between greed and skill. The onus of distinguishing the two lies squarely with the Gun. If he regards the quarry as not sufficiently demanding he should not shoot at it, although any low bird suspected of being 'pricked' or diseased should, of course, be dispatched.

At very close quarters a bird may be so smashed as to be inedible. A high bird at the limit of range may demand great skill to shoot, but the risks of only pricking it are greater. Good judgement is not always easy. An indifferent shot would certainly be forgiven for not shooting at extremely high birds on the borderline of the killing range.

Degree of skill varies. All a Gun can do is to develop his to its highest peak. It may also vary from day to day. The important thing for a Gun to appreciate is not so much the extent of his skill as the limitations of it. Hares and wild geese, particularly, seem to tempt many people to shoot when out of range.

Certain types of shooting require a great deal of fieldcraft and woodcraft, as well as strict adherence to the code of behaviour. This comes with experience.

Choosing the right gun for the right job is important; it is sensible for a beginner to obtain a gun which fits perfectly and to learn how to use it properly. There are ample shooting schools at which to practise. Many experienced shots go back to such schools regularly before each season opens.

The behaviour of a Gun to his fellow sportsmen is as important as his attitude to his quarry. It does not matter whether the sport is wildfowling, rough shooting, grouse driving or stalking. The need for considerate behaviour increases with the formality of the occasion and is at its highest during a driven shoot. But the basic attitude should be the same.

For example, no Gun should dream of turning up unsuitably or inadequately dressed, whatever the occasion: inappropriately bright

A high pheasant clean killed, well in front

Driven grouse coming towards the butt

colours can scare the game and to wear them would display ignorance and bad manners. Nor would a guest commit the cardinal sins of being late and delaying moving off, or leaving a vehicle where it might interfere with the sport.

He should have sufficient cartridges. His dog must be a credit, not a liability. He is courteous to host, fellow Guns, keepers, beaters and to everyone else met during the day. He knows and follows the Code of the Countryside, closing farm gates and avoiding damage to crops or disturbance to livestock. Those who have worked hard to make the day enjoyable and successful should be thanked and, where appropriate, tipped. The host or one of the regular Guns will always give advice on this point.

A wise Gun never questions instructions given, other than seeking to make their meaning absolutely clear. Nor does he complain even if, say, on a driven day, only a few birds come over him but large numbers swarm over his neighbour. Even on the best-run shoots luck plays its part.

Safe behaviour is a vital part of good sportsmanship: see chapter seven, 'Safety and Security'. When in line talk as little or as quietly as possible; ensure that your dog is under tight control and do not move from peg or butt during a drive. When walking from stand to stand between drives endeavour to help others – particularly older people. Ditches and fences can be difficult to negotiate.

On formal shooting occasions much embarrassment can be avoided by making adequate preparations beforehand. This involves the organizer as much as the Guns. Before arrival, a guest will need to know whether to bring one gun or two, a dog (a point which requires tact), a picnic lunch and so on. It will also be sensible to find out whether a wife or a girlfriend will be welcome. The Gun will also need to know exactly where to go and when, throughout the day.

Other information can be given on the spot. It may include the signals to start and finish a drive and, apart from normal legal and seasonal restrictions, what may or may not be shot on a particular day in question. This may depend on local circumstances and it is up to the host to spell them out. Some hosts may not want hares shot or woodcock, golden plover, or other species for that matter.

Foxes should not be shot, unless there is a specific request from your host to do so. It is all too easy to sour relations between the local Hunt and the shooting fraternity. In these days when people tend *either* to shoot *or* to hunt – whereas in earlier times many country people did both – it is essential to try to understand the other's point of view.

Shooting demands instant reactions. In the heat of the moment the mind must prompt the body to do certain things and prevent certain others. When a quarry appears the Gun must make a number of decisions quickly:

i Whether or not the law and your host allows it to be shot.

ii If so, should one leave it to another Gun? Nothing is more annoying to a sportsman than 'poaching' by a neighbour. A good rule of thumb is: would the course the quarry is taking provide another Gun with a better shot? If there is any doubt leave it for him. Your turn will come.

If both Guns fire and the quarry falls it is tactful to credit it to your neighbour, whatever you think!

iii The most important factor to determine – and this point will be repeated many times in this book – is whether the shot is *safe*. If there is anything worse than a Gun who 'poaches' birds it is one who shoots dangerously near his neighbour.

The tally of each Gun is not a point for discussion in Britain. Abroad it may be different. There is a tendency for some Guns to compare numbers killed with cartridges fired. There is no harm in this, providing that efforts to improve an average are not at the expense of sporting considerations or good manners.

The question of retrieving game is vital. No time or effort should be spared. All shot quarry should be collected and wounded game accounted for as quickly as possible. Some Guns take great pride in using their own dogs and enjoy it as much or more than the actual shooting. It is up to the young Gun to make sure that his dog is competent, steady and generally well behaved. If a dog runs in every time it sees a hare it is of little interest that it may have an outstandingly good nose.

On a well-run shoot the host will always ensure enough 'pickers-up'. This is not an area for economizing. Even if most of the guest Guns bring their dogs there is rarely time after every drive to search thoroughly for every bird lost in thick cover, as well as any birds that may have been hard-hit and travelled on a long way.

Dogs are used to 'point' game when walking-up, to flush game from thick cover and also to hunt for, and retrieve, game that may lie hidden or that may be wounded and have run some distance before stopping. Shot game may fall across a river or into water where it could not be retrieved without dog or boat. A well-trained gundog can be a very great asset to the shooting man, provide a great deal of pleasure and, most important, enable a thorough search to be made for any wounded game. In one Scandinavian country, when young sportsmen are tested for their shooting certificate, they are also obliged to bring their gundogs with them. After the general examination the gundog is required to undertake various tasks. If it does not carry these out to the satisfaction of the judge, the *owner* of the dog is failed.

6

Dispatching Wounded Game Humanely[1]

No hunter should be allowed to use a weapon against any type of quarry unless he knows how to dispatch a wounded bird or animal speedily and painlessly. Unfortunately, even with all the care and consideration possible, game cannot always be clean killed.

A description in words of the most effective methods recommended is no substitute for learning at first hand from an expert, so do not be ashamed to ask for demonstrations. Dealing correctly with wounded game is largely a question of knack. Young people can acquire experience of most ways of carrying out the *coup de grâce* by practising on dead specimens that have been freshly shot, after watching an expert carrying out the task.

As has already been said (in the previous chapter) any delay in bringing wounded game to hand should be minimized by the use of well-trained gundogs. It is desirable *not* to leave a wounded bird lying in the open until the end of a drive, but it may often be too dangerous for either man or dog to move out of the line in order to retrieve the quarry. There are occasions when this can be done safely, but *no risks whatever should be taken*. Nearby Guns should be made aware of what you are doing.

Poking about in thick cover behind the Guns is another matter. You are even more likely to put yourself in danger. You may be interfering with the next drive and, in any case, an animal lying hidden in undergrowth never shows the same fear as one out in the open. There is a good deal of medical evidence to show that the shock effect with accompanying numbness lasts several minutes: sometimes for a considerable period.

1. This chapter was originally published as a leaflet by the Game Conservancy to whom grateful acknowledgement is made.

Do not allow misplaced pride to prevent you from firing a second shot at a 'runner' on the ground, if that is the only way of stopping and killing it. In this case make sure that the shot is a safe one and that no dog is running in.

Some of the Most Effective Methods

Gamebirds Two main methods are employed. First, a sharp and powerful blow on the back of the head which will fracture the cranium or sever the spinal cord. Death is virtually instantaneous. When using this technique it is essential that the bird is correctly positioned before the blow is delivered. In some cases a wounded gamebird may be sufficiently active to necessitate holding its wings together above the back to immobilize it and bringing the head into a suitable position for an accurate blow. A heavy stick of convenient length or a 'priest' (see below) is required for the purpose. Sometimes it may be more convenient to swing the bird's head sharply against a hard object, such as a wooden gatepost, tree trunk or large flint. Aim should be careful and deliberate.

Secondly, the spinal cord can be severed by dislocation of the neck where it joins the cranium. There are two ways of undertaking this. Most commonly the bird is grasped by its head and swung round vigorously once. During the swing a quick pull upwards or a sideways jerk will effect dislocation. Practice is required or the head will become detached. (This method is not suitable for small birds, such as woodcock, because they do not generate enough momentum in the swing.) Alternatively, the head may be held firmly and jerked upwards *and backwards* in one quick movement.

Some keepers will humanely dispatch a young bird with a soft skull-bone by fracturing it with a thumb, but this method spoils the appearance for market and looks crude: it is not recommended.

'Priests' Fishermen will be conversant with the short, lead-weighted stick used to kill fish by means of a blow on the head without spoiling their appearance. These can also be used out shooting. We can understand that experts do not need them and also that it is one extra item to carry – along with guns, cartridges, shooting stick, game bag, dog lead, earplugs and so on. We suggest, however, that more sportsmen should give them a trial. Pickers-up could also be issued with them by the host and a spare 'priest' carried in one of the shooting vehicles.

Wildfowl Because of their longer necks wild duck are somewhat less easy to deal with than gamebirds. For the average sportsman a sharp blow to the head is easier to administer than neck dislocation.

Wild geese can be even more difficult. An effective method of dealing with a tough old goose, however, is to lay its head carefully on hard ground, place a stout stick across the back of the neck and stand on either side of the stick to trap the bird securely. The neck – now at right angles to the head – can be dislocated with a sharp upward pull. This is most easily done when holding the bird by its feet. If shooting out on soft mudflats or boggy ground a 'priest' is the only alternative, or a second carefully aimed shot if there is any doubt about one's expertise.

Rabbits and Hares Rabbits and *young* hares can be effectively dealt with by a sharp blow to the back of the head at the joint between neck and cranium. This fractures the spinal cord and life is extinguished instantly. The method entails holding the animal firmly by the hind legs and allowing the body to hang downwards. The blow can be given with the bony, outer edge of the palm – or a stout stick may be used. For old hares, which have considerably tougher necks, some such hard object is definitely necessary to save damage to the hand.

Alternatively, rabbits and hares may have their necks dislocated. This involves a little more skill than the first method and, in the case of hares, much more strength on the part of the operator. Unless one has long arms and strong muscles it *can* be difficult to dispatch an old hare. The alternative is as described above – the sharp blow on the back of the neck, taking care to hold the legs very firmly indeed. Or skilfully, and with assured aim, the hare may be swung in a sufficient arc so that the blow of striking the back of the head against a stout gatepost or tree trunk will be a mortal one. This requires some expertise and the right hard object to be at hand. The 'priest' is virtually foolproof if the hare is held sufficiently firmly.

The technique required for dislocating the necks of rabbits and leverets requires the animal to be held head downwards by the hind legs. The other hand is used to grasp the head firmly behind the ears – a vice being formed by thumb and fingers. At the same moment as the head is turned deftly at right angles to the body it should also be sharply jerked down towards the ground. Expertly done, only a small sudden movement is necessary to cause instantaneous death.

Whatever type of *coup de grâce* is used it is essential to check that the method has been effective and that the animal is dead.

Deer Provided that a suitable rifle and ammunition are chosen and care taken to shoot with knowledge and precision and at reasonable ranges, any deer should be killed outright with the first shot. A shot should *never* be taken (at an *unwounded* beast) unless you are sure of a humane, instant kill.

If, despite every effort, a deer is wounded, a second shot should be taken *at once*. If it lies down or disappears, the stalker should wait at least ten minutes (except in the case of a broken leg) and then approach, taking the greatest care not to be seen or heard. A deer shot in the body will quickly lie down if undisturbed, and die or at least stiffen up. If roused immediately it may go a long way before lying down again. If any life remains a mercy shot in the upper part of the neck should be taken at short range in preference to any amateur attempt with a knife. Only with an injured leg should pursuit, preferably with a dog, start straight away.

The use of experienced tracking dogs can be of value in woodland stalking.

7
Safety and Security

If the traditional pattern of shooting in Britain is to continue, strict obedience to safety rules will be one of the most important considerations. Not only must we observe those which are legally binding, but also the many unwritten laws which have been evolved gradually to protect the public, the shooter and his dog.

In such a comparatively small and, in places, overpopulated country the safety and peace of mind of *all* the users of the land must at all times be of concern: not only farmers and foresters, but ramblers, birdwatchers and picnickers, as well as those engaged in our own or other field sports, such as beaters, ghillies, stalkers or boatmen. Much shooting is carried out in remote places but even when alone the sportsman must never relapse into carelessness, thinking that there is no one else for miles around. Under such circumstances injury to himself or some other person can be followed by a long delay in receiving medical attention.

Always err on the side of safety when in doubt and persevere with safety measures until they become second nature. Remain alert and self-disciplined and exercise common sense: it is easy to let one's standards deteriorate when cold and tired. Do not assume that your shooting companions are necessarily safe; and beware of picking up bad habits from so-called friends. Just because an older or a generally steady person behaves in a certain way, do not assume that it must be correct. In time experience will guide you and you will be able to guide others.

Never shoot without adequate insurance cover.

Conduct in the Field

Never shoot where you cannot see! Cover may conceal a beater, a stop, a picker-up with his dog, or somebody out for a country walk or having a nap under a hedge.

Do not shoot towards highways, public footpaths within range, or towards farmhouses or other dwellings. While it may be quite safe to shoot standing near somebody's cottage, check that you will not be frightening anybody by doing so.

Let the farming staff know when and where you will be shooting. Some of them may be working nearby and in potential danger.

On an organized shoot make sure that you know the allotted positions of the other Guns. Your shooting companions must also be aware of your exact position. Do not assume that your host or the shoot organizer has already told them. And do not hesitate to ask him to explain anything that is not absolutely clear to you.

When rough shooting or fowling on the foreshore, always enquire if any other shooters are in the vicinity. Wildfowling can involve a sportsman in special dangers; see chapter fourteen, 'Wildfowling Today'.

Keep in a straight line when walking with guns and beaters.

Beware of ricochets when shooting low-flying or ground game or across water. And remember the range or carrying power of your ammunition. Small shot may travel over 270yds(250m.)

Do not hesitate, or be too polite, to warn any Gun who may be behaving dangerously, *immediately* before he has a chance to fire another shot.

Check your barrels frequently for blockages. Snow or mud can cause a burst and you could lose a hand.

Never use a gun – perhaps a borrowed weapon – unless you clearly understand its operating mechanism, especially in relation to safety catches and self-loading weapons.

Do not shoot while under the influence of alcohol or medicines which may cause drowsiness or other such conditions. Never shoot unless fully fit: if overcome by illness you may cause an accident.

Gun Handling

Check if a gun is loaded – your own or somebody else's – as soon as you pick it up, whenever you put it in a vehicle, in a gun slip or case, or on entering a house. Everyone forgets to unload at some time.

Never point a gun at anyone, even if unloaded.

Close your gun after loading by bringing the stock upwards while keeping the barrels pointing safely to the ground.

Always unload your gun when negotiating a ditch, hedge, fence or other obstacle. It is not enough to break the gun: take the cartridges out as well.

When in company always carry the empty gun over the crook of your arm, with the breech open.

Always open the breech and unload before passing a gun to someone and always pass the stock first. If possible pass it across closed, but show the person you are handing it to that it is empty.

When carrying an unbroken gun in the course of shooting carry it in any of the following ways:

  i With the breech resting on the shoulder – the trigger guards uppermost – and the barrels pointing skywards.
 ii Over the crook of your arm with barrels pointing to the ground.
iii Held firmly with both hands and the barrels pointing forward and towards the ground.

When waiting in the line or when walking-up game, only point your gun where you are looking and where it is absolutely safe. When turning in a line of Guns to take a shot behind, always point the muzzle skywards: never swing your gun 'through the line'.

Only load a gun when you are about to start shooting.

Never release the safety catch until you are mounting the gun and certain that you will fire it. *A sudden jarring can cause a gun to fire even when on 'safe'.* Always put the gun back on safe between shots. Do not put the safety catch off when you see a distant bird approaching. It may change its direction and no time is lost by waiting until you are mounting the gun.

When expecting to shoot always keep the forefinger along the trigger guard or in some equally safe position – and not inside it near the trigger.

When unloading at the end of a drive turn round with your back to the beaters, covert, etc. and point the barrels to the ground while so doing.

Never stand your gun where it may slip or be accidentally knocked over.

With pump-action or self-loading guns always carry the slide or action open.

Never shoot unless you are well-balanced on both feet and otherwise secure.

Hammer guns are potentially more dangerous weapons, so take extra care with them because wet or cold fingers may easily cause a premature discharge.

Always open a hammer gun and remove the cartridges before uncocking, while pointing the barrels at the ground. Never uncock hammers onto loaded chambers.

Driven-Game Shooting

Although we have recommended that a Gun should not move from the position allocated to him by the shoot organizer, a slight adjustment may be in order if within sight of all and approved by the host.

Be very wary of curved lines of guns when determining safe firing angles. This is especially dangerous in grouse shooting where the Guns may also be at varying heights on the side of a hill. In a straight line of butts shoot only within 45 degrees to the left and right of a line to your front.

Markers on butts are good reminders of the safety limits and physical obstructions such as bamboo rods are even better.

Always unload between drives. Put your empty gun in a sleeve if you have one. It will also protect your weapon.

Make sure you know from which direction the beaters will approach as well as the exact positions of the stops, flankers and pickers-up. The latter often stand close behind the line and may move about.

If you are shooting with a pair of guns, you and your loader should practise with unloaded weapons before shooting begins. The gun should be handed to you and returned with the safety catch 'on'. If, after firing one shot only, the shooter intends to pass the gun back to his loader, he should put the safety catch on again.

Grouse and partridges frequently fly low and towards the end of a drive the beaters can be in danger.

Woodcock will also sometimes fly at head height and change direction quickly. They can cause much excitement and are notorious as the cause of accidents.

Whilst this point does not quite come into the safety category, remember that shooting at pigeons before the start of the drive proper can sometimes ruin a drive. Your host should advise you.

Rough Shooting

Make sure you know exactly where you are allowed to go and where the boundaries are on each piece of land you plan to visit.

Remember – especially when grouse are flying low – that beaters may be approaching over a ridge

Ascertain precisely where your companions and their dogs are and observe the necessary safe shooting angles. Never shoot if in doubt.

Do not fire your gun unduly near to livestock for you may cause distress, resulting in complications such as slipped calves, reduced milk yields and so on.

Hares

Hare drives often attract Guns who shoot only once or twice a year. Such people need discreet watching for they are likely to swing right through the line in their excitement. A firm but tactful briefing at the start of the day is advisable.

Gundogs

Never tie them to yourself or to your shooting stick.

Never take a dog shooting in company unless it is under control and always keep your eye on your dog when using it to flush game out of cover.

The Gun

Read chapter eleven, 'Gun Care and Cleaning', and have your gun overhauled annually to ensure it is maintained in a safe condition. As a precaution check the condition of any gun you may borrow. Your best friend's standards may not be as high as your own.

Remember that in Britain any new or second-hand weapon sold has to meet the standards laid down by the Proof Laws; see chapter eight, 'Sporting Guns and Cartridges'.

Ensure that there is no undue movement between the barrels and the action. This is called 'off the face' and can be dangerous, for when the gun is fired back pressure can develop and escape through the gap, causing serious injury to the eyes.

Never use a gun with badly dented or pitted barrels, or which has developed a sensitive 'hair' trigger which will go off at the slightest touch, or has a faulty safety catch.

The Cartridge

Never mix up the ammunition of different bore guns. For instance, a 20 bore cartridge loaded into a 12 bore by mistake will not fall right through and will allow a 12 bore cartridge to be loaded behind it, probably resulting in a burst barrel and a seriously injured hand.

Be particularly cautious with reloads. Use only cartridges that you have loaded yourself, never exceeding the recommended loads. Do not attempt reloading without the benefit of sound advice and training; see also chapter eight, 'Sporting Guns and Cartridges'.

In the event of a misfire, point the barrels in a safe direction while opening the gun to investigate the cause.

Ensure that your cartridges conform to the Proof limitations of your gun; see chapter eight, 'Sporting Guns and Cartridges'.

Do not store cartridges under extreme conditions of temperature or humidity. High and dangerous pressures can result. These can also be caused if you dry out wet cartridges near undue heat.

Unreasonably large amounts of ammunition should not be stored in one place because of the obvious risk. Store under lock and key.

Whenever possible pick up the empty cases and take them home or put them down a deep rabbit hole. Apart from being unsightly they can be picked up by animals and possibly cause internal injuries – although no fatalities are so far known to have occurred.

Security in the Home

Never have a loaded gun in your house.

Do not leave any gun within reach of children and, in particular, never store ammunition near any guns if there is any chance that they may be accessible to children. Air weapons can also be lethal.

Whenever possible keep your guns in a locked cabinet (preferably of steel) or at least out of sight. Concealment can be a form of security. If a rack is used it should be fitted with a locking device.

If they are not locked away, always dismantle your guns for storage.

Never advertise the whereabouts of your guns – especially valuable ones: it may attract criminals.

Never leave your guns in an unoccupied house for long periods.

Any display guns, e.g. on walls, should be adapted so that they cannot be fired.

Take a note of your gun numbers and photograph guns if they have individual characteristics. This will help if they are stolen. As to rifles, the bolt should be stored separately from the weapon itself.

When Travelling

Always transport your gun in a case or cover.

Never travel with a loaded gun under any conditions.

Try not to leave a gun in an unattended car. If you are obliged to do so conceal it from view, lock all doors and shut the windows.

Never shoot from a *moving* vehicle: a sudden bump can cause an accidental discharge as well as damage the gun.

'A Father's Advice'

If a sportsman true you'd be
Listen carefully to me.
Never, never let your gun
Pointed be at any one;
That it may unloaded be
Matters not the least to me.
When a hedge or fence you cross
Though of time it cause a loss,
From your gun the cartridge take
For the greater safety sake.
If 'twixt you and neighbouring gun
Bird may fly or beast may run,
Let this maxim e'er be thine;
'Follow not across the line.'

Stops and beaters, oft unseen,
Lurk behind some leafy screen;
Calm and steady always be;
'Never shoot where you can't see.'
Keep your place and silent be;
Game can hear and game can see;
Don't be greedy, better spared
Is a pheasant, than one shared.
You may kill, or you may miss,
But at all times think of this –
'All the pheasants ever bred
Won't repay for one man dead.'

These lines were written by the late Mark Beaufoy, MP, for his son Henry M. Beaufoy, on reaching the age of thirteen. They have stood the test of time.

8

Sporting Guns and Cartridges

Guns

The guns used for game and wildfowl shooting in Britain are single and double guns of 4, 8, 10, 12, 16, 20, 28 and .410-bore.[1]

The 4-bore is rare and obsolete, production of the ammunition having ceased. The 8-bore is obsolescent and it is a matter for conjecture how long it will be before the 10-bore follows it.

A few punt guns are in use for wildfowling afloat. They are limited to $1\frac{1}{4}$ins(32mm) bore and fire up to about $\frac{3}{4}$lb(0.34kg) of shot.

The overwhelmingly popular gun for field and wildfowl shooting is the double-barrelled, hammerless, side-by-side 12-bore. A minority of sportsmen prefer the over-and-under version which is popular in Europe, but in the UK this is used chiefly for target shooting. As designed for game shooting, both these guns have $2\frac{1}{2}$ins(64mm) or $2\frac{3}{4}$ins(70mm) chambers to take cartridges of those nominal maximum lengths, and they weigh between $6-6\frac{3}{4}$lbs(2.7–3kg). The over-and-unders are usually somewhat heavier than strictly comparable side-by-sides.

The guns used by the great majority of sportsmen in Britain are either Anson and Deeley type boxlocks or sidelocks. In the former, the

1. This classification, which is used internationally, is derived from the weight of a lead ball which will accurately fit the bore. If twelve such balls go to the pound, then the gun is a 12-bore; if twenty-eight, then the gun is a 28-bore, and so on. The only exception is the .410, which is the actual bore diameter as a decimal fraction of an inch.

The nominal bore diameters of the above mentioned guns are:

4-bore	.935ins	16-bore	.662ins
8	.835	20	.615
10	.775	28	.550
12	.729	.410	.410

percussion mechanism is accommodated in slots machined out of a solid action body. In the latter, the corresponding mechanism is carried on detachable side-plates which are let into the head of the stock and the sides of the action.

The boxlock makes the cheaper gun and the sidelock the more elegant – and more costly. Both are fundamentally sound designs.

Those who can afford them invariably use ejector guns in which the spent cartridge cases are automatically ejected when the gun is opened after firing. The non-ejector, in which they have to be withdrawn by hand, is acceptable and often used, although it is slower to reload.

Double or single triggers may be used, the former being preferred on the score of simplicity and freedom from trouble, and the facility they offer for instant choice of right barrel or left; see also under **'Choke'**.

There has recently been something of a revival of interest in fine hammer guns but, being prone to inadvertent discharge by inexpert manipulation, they are not considered suitable for beginners.

Repeaters, that is, pump guns and the recoil or gas-operated self-loaders (incorrectly known as automatics[1]), are regarded with marked disfavour in Britain and are virtually barred in organized game shooting. Wildfowlers and other solitary shooters, however, can justifiably use them against quarry species, though recent legislation requires that the *total cartridge capacity must be limited to three* – two in the magazine and one in the breech. Magazines can be restricted by means of a special plug, which should be correctly fitted. The new Countryside legislation is at present less clear as to whether a repeater need be stopped off at three cartridges when shooting pests proved to be damaging crops. But until clarification is obtained, it would be most unwise to assume that it is legal to exceed three rounds.

It should be noted that the self-loaders are more prone to breakdown than double guns and have a shorter trouble-free life; also that they are much inferior to them on the score of safety. This arises from the lack of any comparable facility for inspecting the bores or for unloading on every occasion when considerations of safety make it desirable.

Lighter guns of smaller bore than the popular 12 are used but, although they have their supporters, they are chiefly used by older men, boys and ladies. The 16-bore is almost the same as the 12-bore in terms of effective range, but the 20, 28 and .410 are considerably lighter and, taking smaller cartridges with lighter shot loads, have a shorter effective range.

Larger-bore guns firing heavy charges are used by wildfowlers for long-range shooting at duck and geese; but the use of these guns is fast

1. Automatics are illegal; repeaters require a separate trigger pull for each shot.

diminishing on account of the very high cost of the ammunition and the limited number of manufacturers of it. Another factor is the increased availability of magnum 12-bore guns and ammunition with almost as heavy shot loads – up to $1\frac{7}{8}$oz(53.5g) of shot, compared with the $1-1\frac{1}{8}$oz(28–32g) of the normal game loads.

A gun of arguably superior merit is the light 12-bore with 2ins(50mm) chambers, firing a special cartridge loaded with $\frac{7}{8}$oz(25g) of shot. These guns have been highly commended for driven partridge shooting and the like, but they are something of a British speciality; in Europe 32g, even 36g, loads are preferred for game shooting, partly because of the tradition of shooting walked-up birds at longer ranges.

The Weight of Guns

In choosing a gun, weight needs careful consideration, not only in relation to the strength and stamina of the shooter, but also for the limitation of recoil and the stresses imposed on the gun itself by firing. The old rule of thumb is that the gun should weigh not less than ninety-six times the weight of the shot charge, or 6lb(2.7 kg) of gun for every 1oz(28g) of shot. Thus a 12-bore gun firing the normal game load of $1\frac{1}{16}$oz(30g) of shot should weigh about $6\frac{1}{2}$lb(3kg). Differences in recoil-tolerance and in the number of cartridges likely to be fired in close succession admit of limited elasticity in the interpretation of this rule.

Some of the self-loaders, notably the gas-operated kind, give an abnormally light feeling of recoil and may be acceptable for use with somewhat heavier loads than those normally associated with their weight. Incorrectly adjusted recoil-operated guns, however, can give rise to excessive recoil. Gun headache can follow.

Fitting a Gun

The novice should make sure that his gun is a reasonable fit. The stock must be of the correct length – not long enough to catch the clothing or so short that the thumb or fingers can catch the tip of the nose when the gun recoils. Too short a stock can cause bruising of the second finger by the trigger guard.

When the gun is mounted the butt must rest fully and fairly in the shoulder recess. The comb, that is, the upper part of the stock, must rest snugly and firmly in the angle between the cheekbone and the jaw; and, these conditions being satisfied, the dominant or master eye must be in line with the rib and just above it.

The novice should always seek the advice of a competent gunsmith to ensure that his gun is a correct fit in accordance with the above requirements. Such a gunsmith can make any necessary alterations to the stock.

Cartridges and Loads

Shotgun cartridges have three essential functions:

i They have to act as a container, preferably waterproof, for the components of the charge, namely, the powder, shot, wadding and cap.

ii They have to restrain the emergence of the shot until the powder is thoroughly ignited.

iii They have to seal the breech against the pressure of the propellent gases.

Modern British cartridges are usually made with plastic (polyethylene) cases, crimp-closed and with a waterproof seal, though paper cases are available in certain brands and are preferred by those shooters who consider the paper to possess some ballistic merit by virtue of its greater compressibility as compared with polyethylene. This is believed to promote more regular pressures. There are also those who prefer paper to plastic on environmental grounds.

The wads in normal game cartridges are made of felt substitute, though one-piece plastic wads incorporating a shot protector are also available. The claim to superiority of these latter wads is based on better shot patterns and is probably only valid for shooting at long ranges.

Powder is nowadays always of the smokeless kind, unless black powder is specified for use in one of the older guns which has never been nitro-proved; see **'Proof'** below. Modern powders are based on nitro-glycerine and gelatinized or fibrous nitro-cellulose.

In recent years there has been a marked revival in the home-loading of cartridges for field and practice clay-pigeon shooting. Home-loaded cartridges can be quite satisfactory provided they are loaded with care and strictly in conformity with the instructions laid down by ammunition manufacturers and other authorities.[1]

It should be particularly noted that dangerous pressures can easily be set

1. Eley Ammunition Dept publish an excellent instructional leaflet for this purpose and there has recently appeared a British book, *Cartridge Loading* by David Garrard, published by Percival Marshall of London, which should be studied by anyone contemplating the regular loading of his cartridges.

up in home-loaded cartridges which depart, even in what may appear to be insignificant respects, from the recommended loads.

Modern British cartridges offer a range of loads in the popular gauges for various kinds of shooting. Thus, for field-shooting, there are loads available for 12-bores ranging from $\frac{7}{8}$oz(25g) for the 2ins(50mm) chambered gun to $1\frac{1}{8}$oz(32g) for the $2\frac{1}{2}$ins(64mm). For wildfowling there are $1\frac{1}{4}$oz(35g) loads for $2\frac{3}{4}$ins(70mm) chambers and up to $1\frac{5}{8}$oz(46g) for 3ins(76mm). Other loads are available for the smaller and larger bores.

Beginners should beware of the delusion that success in shooting is largely proportional to the weight of the shot charge used. Within wide limits it is much more dependent on the suitability and quality of the patterns thrown; see '**Patterns**' and '**Shot Size and Effective Range**' below. Because too much is often expected of them, cartridges carrying extra heavy or 'magnum' loads are a frequent source of disappointment.

Beginners should take careful note of the length of their cartridges, as hitherto denoted by the length of the unloaded (or fired) case. It was a rigid rule that this should never exceed the length of the chamber. Since crimp closures became common, however, the length of the cartridge has been denoted by the length of the chamber for which the cartridges are designed, as stated on the carton. *They must never be used in chambers of any lesser length.*

Choke

Choke is the name given to a constriction of the bore at the muzzle end of a gun barrel. Its purpose is to give an inward impulse to the outside pellets of the charge, whereby it is more concentrated in flight and makes a smaller pattern circle than that thrown by a barrel lacking any such constriction. This concentration of the charge extends the effective range of the gun by increasing the distance to which patterns of a killing density can be thrown. At the same time the reduced spread makes greater demands on the marksmanship of the shooter for the realization of its theoretical advantage – demands which are by no means always met. Long experience has accordingly shown that the most advantageous degree of choke is the least degree consistent with the requirements of the sport concerned. Game guns normally require very little choke; but wildfowling guns regularly used against duck and geese at extreme range can justifiably carry very tight chokes.

Table 1 opposite gives the definition of the various degrees of choke and nominal values of the corresponding patterns and spread. It should be particularly noted that the effective degree of choke in ready-made guns is often greater than that given in the sales specification.

The degree of choke usually favoured for a 12-bore gun designed for general rough shooting in Great Britain is improved cylinder in the right barrel and half to three-quarters choke in the left. If the gun is required chiefly for driven-game shooting it is usually advantageous to have both barrels bored improved cylinder, or only quarter choke in the left. Note that double triggers are especially advantageous when there is much difference between the choke in the two barrels.

Patterns

Patterns, as already indicated, are usually defined by the number of pellets expressed as a percentage of the total charge, thrown into a 30ins(760mm) diameter circle at a range of 40yds(37m). Too much attention is commonly paid to this percentage and not enough to the uniformity of distribution as between the central and peripheral parts of the pattern, and the freedom from voids or open patches. Merit and percentage do not march together; it should always be remembered that most game is shot between 20–30 yards and that the most effective pattern, taking one shot with another, is likely to be the one best adapted to this range bracket, for which very little choke is needed. Excessive choke is the bane of many young shooters.

Table 1

Type of boring	Nominal percentage pattern in 30ins circle at 40yds	Nominal diameter of spread of bulk of pattern at various distances		
		20yds	30yds	40yds
True cylinder	40	32ins	44ins	58ins
Improved cylinder	50	26	38	51
$\frac{1}{4}$ choke	55	23	35	48
$\frac{1}{2}$ choke	60	21	32	45
Full choke	70	16	27	40

Shot Size and Effective Range[1]

Shotguns kill by a combination of shock and damage. In this context, shock is defined as the severe depression of an animal's vital forces caused

1. Abstracted with permission from an article by the author in the 1979 edition of *The Shooter's Diary*, published by Eley.

by the impact on its nervous system of multiple injuries, individually not necessarily serious.

Damage is injury to one or more vital organs whereby they cease to function adequately to sustain or preserve life. The proportionate contribution of these two causes of death may vary from case to case.

As shotgun pellets cannot be individually aimed it is necessary to strike the target with a sufficient number to make it reasonably certain that the resulting shock and damage will together bring about a clean kill.

This requires that the pattern density and penetrative power – that is, the striking energy – of the individual pellets shall be adapted to the size, weight, vitality and protective covering of the quarry; and, since pattern density and pellet energy diminish with increasing distance, it also requires that, with a given gun and load, the range shall not exceed the 'effective' range, this being the greatest range at which a fatal combination of shock and damage is likely to be inflicted by a truly aimed shot.

The best size of shot to use for this purpose in a given case cannot be laid down: guidance can be offered only in general terms. Reducing the size of the pellets increases the number in the charge. It thus increases the probable number of hits and, therefore, the shock component, as well as the chance of finding a vital spot. It also notably improves the consistency of results from one shot to another at normal range. At the same time, the smaller size of the pellets means that, individually, they have less penetrative power and so a lower damage potential.

Too large a size, on the other hand, though capable of scoring kills by fluke at extreme range, is incapable of consistent results at what should be normal full reach, because of the unduly open patterns and therefore the wide variation from one shot to another in the number of hits. The practical limits of compromise, as accepted by the majority of experienced shooters, are fairly reflected in the following table:

Table 2

Game	Shot size
Geese	BB, 1 or 3
Hare	4 or 5
Wild duck	4, 5 or 6
Rabbit	5 or 6
Pheasant	5, 6 or 7
Pigeon	6 or 7
Grouse, partridge, teal & woodcock	6 or 7
Snipe	7 or 8

Taking one shot with another, it is advantageous to use the smallest size which will give good penetration as pattern begins to fail.

Effective range is limited fundamentally by the weight of the shot charge and the boring of the gun – not by the *bore*. An ounce of shot, thrown to a good quality pattern by a truly aimed gun with improved cylinder boring, will kill up to 35 yards with reasonable consistency. Every extra $\frac{1}{8}$oz(3.5g) will add about 3 yards to this figure, reducing to 2 at extended range. Half choke will add about 5 yards and full choke about 10 throughout; but, as stated, full choke much increases missing in the 20–30 yard range bracket within which most game is shot.

Shooters are warned against overrating the effective range of their guns and cartridges on the strength of occasional long-range kills. The most successful shooter over a period is the man who places a strictly realistic estimate on the effective range of his gun and cartridges; who has practised as much as possible; who has developed his judgement of distances; who uses no greater degree of choke and no larger pellets than his sport strictly necessitates; and *who never fires when he is in doubt of his ability to reach his game and kill it in a clean and sportsmanlike manner.*

Safety A gun is a source of power, potentially lethal to man and beast. It thus lays a heavy responsibility on its user to observe the safety code unfailingly; see chapter seven, 'Safety and Security'.

Proof

No gun can be lawfully sold or exchanged in Great Britain unless it bears the appropriate proof marks of one or other of the British proof authorities, or those of a foreign country with whom Britain has reciprocal arrangements, and is still 'in proof'. Buyers of used guns should consult a professional gunsmith for verification of the proof status of a proposed purchase. It should be noted that guns proved for black powder only, and still in proof, may lawfully be sold, but that such guns, irrespective of their general condition, must be regarded as potentially dangerous if used with smokeless powder.

Only those cartridges clearly described on the carton as being suitable for use in guns of the appropriate gauge, chamber length and proof status, whether British or foreign, should be used.

Gun Deafness

Only in recent years has the *irreparable* loss of upper-register hearing due to shooting been clearly recognized. Such deafness, however, can be prevented by wearing approved ear-plugs, such as 'Gunfenders', when shooting. Their use is strongly recommended; conversation and wing beats can still be heard but the percussion effect is greatly reduced.

It should be the duty of every parent to insist that the young shot uses ear-plugs from the day he starts shooting, and not when it is too late. Their use is somewhat equivalent to the protection afforded by a crash helmet to a motorcyclist: it is no good after the damage has been done.

9

Air-Weapon Shooting[1]

Few small boys can resist the chance to fire an air rifle, even if only at a fairground, and providing this natural inclination is properly channelled air rifles provide the ideal introduction to shooting sports. The weapon itself need not be expensive, the lead pellets used in it are cheap and it has a limited range. As long as the young beginner is made to realize that an air rifle is a weapon and not a toy he can both acquire shooting skills and learn safety habits which become instinctive.

Parents who allow their children to play with air weapons without proper instruction and supervision are irresponsible. They risk serious accidents to their own and other people's children; a pellet can easily blind a person at over 50yds(45m). Vandalism in the form of 'potting' at unsuitable targets, such as street lights, telegraph insulators, and even protected birds and domestic animals, must also be stamped on ruthlessly. This should be the job of the parent and not the police.

Types of Weapon and Their Use

A few air weapons are gas (CO_2) powered or are of the 'pump-up' variety; from the legal point of view these are regarded in the same light as small-bore rifles if their kinetic energy exceeds certain limits. The vast majority, however, are simply 'cocked' by compressing a powerful spring, either by operating a lever or by 'breaking' the barrel. When the trigger is squeezed the spring is released, forcing the piston up the body of

1. Written in collaboration with Webley & Scott, National Smallbore Rifle Association and Eley Ammunition Dept of IMI Ltd, to whom grateful acknowledgement is made.

the weapon. The air pressure created is transferred to the base of the lead pellet which has been loaded into the breech of the barrel. This principle applies both to air rifles and to air pistols.

Because of the comparatively low power of the pellet an air rifle or pistol range can be set up simly and safely in a room at home, or outside, providing care is taken to provide a solid backstop and to avoid ricochets. This can be ensured by having a timber or earth backstop, or an angled metal pellet 'catcher'.

Both air rifles and air pistols can be used to train young people, but the air pistol is primarily used for target pistol shooting and needs more supervision and skill. Smooth-bore air *guns* were common before the 1939 war, but they lack power and accuracy and are unsuitable for all but elementary target shooting.

Air rifles, produced in two calibres, .177″ (No. 1) and .22″ (No. 2), should be used for sporting purposes; while the .177″ is ideal for target practice and serious target shooting, the .22″ calibre should be the choice of anyone shooting small vermin, since the greater range and knock-down power of the heavier pellet makes it a far more effective and humane weapon.

Legal Use

For use by young persons, see chapter four, 'The Law and Shooting'.

No licence for standard air weapons is required, but some gas-operated or pump-up types fall within the Firearms Act and are treated in the same way as .22 rim-fire weapons if they generate more than 12ft/lb (air rifles) or 6ft/lb (air pistols) kinetic energy.

Effective Range

The average .22″ air-rifle pellet will have a muzzle velocity of 500–550ft (152–168m)/sec. and so its effective range for killing vermin is no more than 25 yards even though the pellet will travel, and still be dangerous, much further than that. To kill humanely at 25 yards requires a considerable degree of accuracy, particularly with larger targets such as squirrels and rabbits, and young people should be required by their parents or supervisors to demonstrate their proficiency on targets before being allowed to shoot at animals. They should be capable of hitting a target in the head with reasonable consistency and without the support of a rest. The risk of wounding must be reduced as much as possible and the temptation of a long shot at a rabbit just outside its burrow should be resisted. Many air rifles are now fitted with telescopic sights and while these can improve the accuracy of the shooting it must be remembered that they do not increase the range!

In the right hands an efficient air rifle can provide a useful means of reducing furred and feathered pests with quiet economy, whether it be sparrows or rats. Because of its valuable role in training the recruit in gun handling, safety precautions and marksmanship, in the minimum area and with the maximum economy, it deserves a place in most gun cupboards.

10

The .22 Rifle

Many young shots progress from air weapons to the .22 rim-fire rifle and there is no better training for using a .22 efficiently and safely than thorough proficiency with an air rifle. What must be realized from the outset is that, although the cartridge looks insignificant, the .22 is a deadly weapon which can, under certain circumstances, kill a man at a distance of one mile. From the outset anyone using a .22 should be constantly aware of this; many people have been killed by this innocuous-looking cartridge. The bullet is much more inclined to ricochet than faster bullets from heavy stalking rifles.

Cartridges

Two basic cartridges are available for the rifle we are considering; that is, the .22 rim-fire rifle with the designation long rifle (LR). These are:

i The .22 short cartridge which is loaded with a 29-grain bullet.
ii The .22 long rifle cartridge with a 35–40-grain bullet.
   (There is also a special .22 cartridge loaded with dust shot, but this will not concern the average sportsman.)

The cartridges listed are interchangeable in one rifle, although the bullets will not necessarily shoot to the same point. They are designated 'rim-fire' (or RF) because the primer is contained in the rim of the cartridge and not in a separate central cap, as in the case of shotgun and larger rifle cartridges. The other rim-fire cartridge, the .22 rim-fire magnum is *not* interchangeable.

Those .22 cartridges, having a *central cap*, come under the general classification of .22 centre-fire (CF) cartridges. Each one of these can only be used in rifles designed and chambered for that particular cartridge.

They are much more powerful than the .22 rim-fire long rifle and are dealt with in the last section of this chapter.

Both the .22 RF long rifle and short cartridges are available in high- or low-velocity loading, and with solid or hollow-pointed bullets. The former are more suited to target, the latter to live quarry in which a hollow-nosed bullet will expand to give a quick, humane kill.

Rifle design is largely a matter of personal choice. Rapid shooting is not part of the careful, sportsmanlike use of a .22: so a magazine, although useful, is not necessary. If a magazine is fitted it should be simple to load and easily inspected to make sure that it has been unloaded. The rifle for sporting purposes should be reasonably light, not a heavy specialized target weapon but with a really accurate barrel, well bedded into the woodwork and with a crisp single-stage trigger capable of adjustment down to a pull of about 2.2lbs(1kg). It must be fitted with a safety catch. Most shooters choose a bolt or lever action, the former being potentially the most reliable and accurate. Self-loading (semi-automatic) rifles are also made but are not recommended, particularly for the beginner. It is very easy to shoot dangerously with them and some are prone to malfunction. The fore-end and stock should be fairly chunky to allow a good steady hold and the rifle should be fitted with a sling so that it can be carried over one shoulder, leaving the hands free for using the binoculars – an essential aid to safe and effective sporting shooting.

Sights

The rifle will come equipped with iron sights, that is, a knob or blade on the front of the barrel which must be aligned with a notch or 'V' in the rear sight, and with the target. These 'open' sights are perfectly effective if correctly zeroed and used in reasonable light at short range.

The 'peep' sight is slower in use but more accurate. In this the rear notch is replaced by a disc with a hole in the centre through which the shooter looks at the foresight and the target. His eye will automatically make use of the centre of this hole, even if it is quite large. Peep sights are usually more easily adjusted than open sights, having screw adjustments for elevation and windage.

Most young shooters will, however, aspire to a telescopic sight which is rigidly clamped to the action of the rifle and in which there is an aiming device (or graticule), often a cross-wire, which appears clearly on the target image, avoiding the difficulty of focusing simultaneously on rear sight, foresight and target. There is no doubt that a well-designed telescopic sight allows one to shoot more accurately and in poorer light, but it is a delicate optical instrument and the cheaper ones particularly can be very easily jarred out of adjustment and must be regularly checked.

Choice of Cartridge

The .22 RF short cartridge makes very little noise and is extremely effective against such quarry as rats, rooks and so on, and rabbits at short range, say up to 27 yards (25 metres). At longer range and for tough species like squirrels, the .22 long-rifle cartridge should be used. Both the short and the long are loaded at standard speed and at high velocity. Particularly with the short cartridge the high-velocity version carries more 'punch', but both have the disadvantage that the bullet is more affected by wind than the slower version. High velocity means flatter trajectory and so range estimation is easier. If you want to shoot rabbits at 80 metres consistently, use the high-velocity load, but expect quite a lot of deflection if the wind gets up. The long rifle standard-velocity load at a speed of 1,025ft(312m)/sec. is just below the speed of sound and therefore has the advantage of not making the miniature sonic boom, heard as a loud crack with all missiles above this speed. For this reason it disturbs game less and if the rifle is fitted with a silencer, a cumbrous but useful tool, almost all the noise of the shot can be eliminated. Possession of a silencer, which has to be screwed to the barrel, needs an amendment to your Firearm Certificate.

Zeroing

Range estimation is important to the .22 sporting rifleman to a much greater degree than is the case with deer stalking. These small bullets drop away very quickly from the line of sight, so the rifle must be zeroed, that is, adjusted to make sure that the bullet hits the spot at a convenient working range. Nearer than that it will shoot slightly high, further off it will be low, and adjustments will have to be made if a small target like a squirrel is to be shot and killed. To give an example, if the rifle is accurate at 50 metres, using the long rifle standard-velocity cartridge, it will be 1.1in(28mm) high at 25 metres, enough to miss a rabbit's head unless a low aiming point is taken. The flatter shooting high-velocity round would be only 0.7in(18mm) high at the same range and a slightly longer 'point blank' might be 60 metres, for example, for this round. Each size, bullet weight, make – and even batch of cartridges – is liable to shoot to a different point. Different lots should not be mixed and the rifle must be re-zeroed when changing from one to another.

Cleaning

Although the residue from modern cartridges will not cause corrosion in the barrel, it does not protect the metal completely from rusting. If the rifle has got wet it must be cleaned, inside and out, and oiled. This oil must also be wiped out before the rifle is used again.

In addition, powder residue builds up in the rifling and must be removed periodically by the use of a properly designed wire brush which has been dipped in cleaning fluid. After this the barrel should be mopped out with a square of flannelette and lightly oiled as before. The action, particularly if the rifle is automatic, can become clogged with powder residue which must also be brushed out from time to time. The exterior of the barrel should be lightly oiled and all screws attaching the metalwork to the stock, or the telescopic sight to the action, should be kept tight.

More Powerful .22 Cartridges

Many cartridges, nominally of .22 calibre, are available but, as has been pointed out above, they are not interchangeable with the normal .22 long rifle rim-fire cartridge nor can they be used in rifles designed for the standard .22 ammunition. Most of these high-power .22 cartridges were developed in the United States of America for their national pastime of 'varmint hunting', the long-range pursuit of pests and predators, from squirrels to wolves.

Next in power to the .22 long rifle is the .22 rim-fire magnum. In spite of its obvious relationship to the long rifle the .22 rim-fire magnum will not fit into the same chamber and is only suitable for rifles intended for this round. It fires a 40-grain bullet at 2,000ft(610m)/sec.

The .22 centre-fire (CF) rifles use bottle-shaped cartridges with a separate cap, similar to a shotgun cartridge in the centre of the head. Great care should be taken that the markings on the cartridge and on the rifle are similar. The fact that a cartridge may fit into a rifle not designed for it does not necessarily mean that it can be used with safety. An example of these accurate, flat-shooting rounds is the .222 Remington which fires a 50-grain bullet at 3,200ft(975m)/sec. In skilled hands it is a deadly weapon for foxes and is used widely in Scotland for roe deer. (No .22 rifle may be used against roe in England and Wales.) The .22 centre-fire rifles should be considered somewhat specialized weapons and the beginner should not be tempted to launch out into ownership before he has, on one hand, fully explored the considerable potential of the .22 rim-fire long rifle and, on the other, of the acknowledged deer-stalking calibres.

11

Gun Care and Cleaning

Shotguns

Following the introduction of smokeless propellants and non-corrosive priming in cartridges the tedious procedure of gun cleaning, previously necessary, can now be modified. Sportsmen should establish a basic cleaning routine and thus ensure *safe functioning* and preservation of valuable shotguns.

On returning from the field, immediately after attending to the needs of any dogs, the gun should be dismantled into its three basic parts of fore-end, barrels and action. A soft cloth or absorbent kitchen paper should be used to remove all traces of moisture, mud or blood from the exterior of the gun. Particular attention should be paid to each side of the top and bottom barrel ribs and all traces of dirt and moisture should be removed, using a folded piece of blotting or absorbent paper. Moisture penetrating under the rib can cause rusting between the barrels, resulting in, at best, an expensive repair and, at worst, a burst barrel.

The bores of the gun are best cleaned by pushing through them several balls of newsprint or other soft paper to remove the bulk of the fouling. Obstinate deposits can be removed using a bristle or phosphor bronze brush on the end of a stout wooden cleaning rod. Do not use a steel 'turks head' brush as this can scratch the surface of the bore and cause 'leading'. The barrels should then be wiped clean with cloth patches on a jag or loop. A light oiling given to the bores, using a good quality gun-oil on a lambswool mop or a *short* spray from an aerosol, will suffice after the barrels are clean. Too much oil will clog the extractors and may run back through the firing-pin holes into the action where it will soak into the head of the stock, reducing its strength.

All traces of dirt and powder fouling should be removed from the surface of the action and fore-end; a suitable feather will be found useful for cleaning round the triggers and under the extractors. Always ensure that the square notches or 'bites' which are cut into the barrel lumps are free from dirt; clean and lightly oil the joint-pin located in the front part of the action on which the barrels hinge.

All moisture and dirt should be removed from the woodwork; dried dirt can be removed from the chequering using an old dry toothbrush. A light application of linseed oil or a good quality wax-polish will restore and enhance the woodwork. Avoid using gun oils on the woodwork unless specifically recommended for it, and keep linseed oil away from the metal working parts – it becomes sticky.

Do's

Always clean your gun as soon after use as possible.

Always use clean, good-quality oil and cleaning materials.

Always examine the gun a few days after cleaning to check that no part has been overlooked.

Be sure to remove all traces of oil from the bore before firing.

Send your gun at the end of each season to your gunsmith to be cleaned and checked for safety.

Don'ts

Never neglect dents in barrels. Have them removed immediately by your gunsmith.

Do not use excess oil as it can contaminate the woodwork, causing weakness and breakages, and accumulate dirt.

Never fire your gun without first checking that the barrels are clear.

Do not attempt to dismantle actions or ejector mechanisms. This is a skill requiring the precision of a gunsmith.

Always remember that guns are rarely worn out by use, more often by abuse.

Only use good quality cartridges loaded specifically for the chamber length of your gun.

I2

Gamebirds and Woodcock

We tend to use the term 'game' loosely; this is not very important unless the law is involved. Wildfowl are not, strictly speaking, game and the hare is defined as 'game' in one Act but not in another. What we are concerned about in this book are all those birds and animals that are legitimate quarry for the sportsman, whether they are legally 'game' or not.

Under the heading of gamebirds are: the pheasant, the common partridge, the red-legged partidge, the red grouse, the black grouse, the capercaillie and the ptarmigan. For the sake of convenience we shall include the woodcock, which is really a wader, in this section. The migratory quail is also, officially, game but it is protected.

Some brief notes concerning these species follow. The shooter should learn to familiarize himself with each one: only so much can be learned from illustrations in books – experience in the field is essential.

Apart from the normal code of practice concerning shooting in general, some game may need special considerations when being pursued as quarry. A few ideas are suggested.

Pheasant (*Phasianus colchicus*)

It seems fairly certain that the Romans first introduced the pheasant to Britain towards the end of their period of occupation. Besides the species we now call the old English black-neck (*Phasianus colchicus*) they probably also brought over Chinese pheasants or 'ringnecks' (*Phasianus c. torquatus*). Many other species were subsequently introduced and all will cross-breed with each other. It is now a common bird almost everywhere.

Pheasant (Phasianus colchicus)

The pheasant favours the edge of woodlands; it is also found on mixed farms and marshy areas. The species does not like softwood forests, particularly when the acreage is extensive. It prefers to walk rather than fly and will roost on the ground if there are no trees or bushes nearby.

The pheasant will eat an extremely wide variety of animal and vegetable foods. In addition to the fruits, seeds and leaves of wild plants and trees, some roots and tubers are consumed and many insects and their larvae.

The breeding season usually begins about mid-February when the cocks start to spar amongst themselves. During March and the first half of April dominant cocks establish breeding territories (4–5 acres or 2 ha.) and this is accompanied by crowing. Cocks without territories do not crow. Hens tend to wander in small groups at this time – mating indiscriminately with different cocks. When egg-laying starts the hens settle in their own individual home ranges which can overlap the territories of several cocks. There is no pair bond.

Egg-laying extends from mid-March to early June, with a peak in late April. The average clutch consists of about twelve olive-coloured eggs which are incubated for twenty-three to twenty-four days by the hen alone. Foxes, stoats and the crow family are the main predators. Should a

Pheasant shooting: an overhead shot by one of the line of Guns strung out across the small valley

nest be destroyed a hen will almost invariably attempt to re-nest in a different place after about ten days.

Most chicks hatch between 18–30 May; the usual brood is ten, quickly reduced by natural hazards and predators. A plentiful supply of insects greatly assists chick survival. Very occasionally a hen will re-lay after losing her brood of young chicks.

The crowing of a cock pheasant is difficult to describe in print; it is usually a two-note utterance, 'Karrk-Karrk', but there are many variants. They will crow noisily before going to roost; this is called 'cocking', and they will also drum loudly with their wings rather like a barnyard rooster.

Special Considerations The wild pheasant population in Great Britain has declined, mostly for the same reasons as the partridge, though pheasants are less dependent on hedgerows for nesting and to some extent on insects as an essential food for the chicks. Other aspects of intensive farming have also contributed to the reduction of their numbers. The pheasant population can, however, be restored by rearing and excellent – virtually natural – hunting be provided. Rearing should not, however, be considered as a cure-all and take the place of wild-game management. The wild stock should be encouraged, whether birds are reared or not.

A walked-up pheasant rising out of wet kale a few yards ahead of the Guns can be of little interest to a good shooter and should be allowed to fly on. The high pheasant curving in the wind can be one of the hardest shots encountered by a demanding sportsman. It is up to the owner or manager of a shoot to show his pheasants so that they are exciting and difficult to shoot. A big bag – mere numbers – is not what the real sportsman should look for – quality comes before quantity.

It is usual to shoot 'cocks only' after Christmas in order to leave sufficient hens for breeding the following year – particularly if the shoot is relying on wild stock. It seems obvious to say that a dead hen pheasant cannot lay eggs the following spring, but too many shooters are more concerned with today than tomorrow.

Partridge

There are two species of partridge in Great Britain: the native Common or Grey partridge (*Perdix perdix*) and the introduced Red-legged partridge (*Alectoris rufa*).

If a bird is in flight or at a distance the inexperienced observer may not be able to distinguish between the two species, but at close range there can be no confusion.

Common or Grey Partridge (*Perdix perdix*)

Up till a generation ago the grey partridge was the shooting man's main quarry: it was commoner than the wild pheasant. Now it is much less plentiful, having been less able to adapt to modern farming as successfully as the pheasant, and also because it is not quite such a suitable subject for replacing by rearing.

Partridge nests (fifteen-sixteen eggs) are often hidden under tufts of grass, by preference along hedgerows; but if these are not available they will nest in crops. The peak hatching date occurs in mid-June. A little over half the nests hatch: the rest are lost to predators, such as foxes, stoats, feral cats and the crow family; or, in the case of nests in crops, to farm machinery.

Usually about fourteen chicks hatch per successful nest but, depending on the weather, half to three-quarters of the young will die. The cause is usually attributable to a poor food supply coupled with inclement weather. A diet of readily available insects such as caterpillars, plant bugs and ants is vital to chick survival; they have to get their food quickly because in cool or wet weather they must spend most of their time being brooded and kept warm by the mother. Insects of the right kind have declined greatly as a result of the use of pesticides. Herbicides have also had an inimical effect as they destroy the plants upon which certain food-

Grey partridge (Perdix perdix)

A partridge is shot, driven over the line of Guns on the downs

insects live. The use of farm chemicals is the main reason for the recent increase in the mortality rate of chicks. Once past the chick stage the young partridges eat unripe weed seeds, buds, other plant foods and, in due course, grain.

Stubble burning, early ploughing and the elimination of 'rough corners' on farms have also contributed to their low numbers.

Partridges spend the autumn and winter in family parties known as 'coveys'. They are well adapted to cold weather and, providing they can find grain on the stubbles, and other suitable vegetable food later on, they can withstand all but the most severe winters. In spring pairing takes place and, if both birds have survived, the pair will re-mate the following year.

A good covey of partridges over the Guns

Young males entice young females from coveys other than their own, whereupon the female begins the search for a suitable nest-site.

The partridge's call is sometimes described as the sound of a key turning in a rusty lock.

Special Considerations The numbers of this declining species are unlikely to increase substantially in view of modern farming methods. But present research concerning partridge food and cover requirements – if sympathetically put into practice – is likely to effect some improvement and provide a reasonable surplus to shoot in some areas in some seasons.

Occasionally, in a really good year when the weather and other conditions have been favourable, a fairly rapid build-up of the partridge population may occur. When this happens good shooting may be enjoyed, though the sportsman should remember that an allowance must be made for the natural winter wastage: at least 30 per cent losses will occur before the following nesting season. Although it is not always possible, the best way to harvest partridges from a conservation point of view is to organize the required number of driving days in October, rather than hunt the birds up and disturb them week after week, continuing on into the pheasant season. Such harassment – with a chance of wounding as the birds get wilder and longer shots are taken – will affect the following year's breeding stock. Grey partridges usually fly over the Guns in coveys. Red-legged partridges tend to come over in twos and threes – sometimes even singly.

Red-legged Partridge (*Alectoris rufa*)

Red-legs – or Frenchmen as they are sometimes called – are most commonly found on farmland, especially where there is a large proportion of arable. They also occur on sandy heaths, chalk downlands and on ground where there is a proportion of scrub.

The winter coveys start to disperse in March and the break-up may extend to early April. The cocks assume breeding territories and some hens associate with a number of cocks before settling down with their final mate. Besides nesting in hedgerows and woodlands, red-legs will occasionally nest off the ground, for example, in a haystack or pollarded tree. Most eggs are laid during May; they are coloured pale buff, speckled with reddish-brown. The clutch size is variable (ten–sixteen eggs), the average being eleven–twelve. As with the grey partridge, repeat clutches replace nests lost in the early stages. Unlike the grey partridge the red-leg

Red-legged partridge (Alectoris rufa)

does not cover the eggs when it leaves the nest and losses due to predation are much heavier. It suffers from more or less the same predators as the pheasant.

Sometimes two clutches are laid by the hen – the first one invariably being incubated and the brood reared independently by the cock. How commonly this occurs is not certain, but a recent Game Conservancy study found that about 30 per cent of the nests on a Norfolk estate were being incubated by cocks. The eggs are extremely 'tough' and can hatch successfully after being abandoned for several weeks, as occurs when the hen is absent laying the second clutch. Normally the cock goes down on his eggs at almost the same time as the hen starts her incubation. The cock develops female characteristics and behaviour whilst he is hatching and brooding. The peak hatching period occurs between the second and fourth weeks in June.

Red-leg chicks are extremely mobile from a few days old and spend more hours per day feeding than grey partridge chicks. For the latter insects are vital during the first few weeks of life – but for red-leg chicks, in certain circumstances, highly nutritional plant food seems to suffice. Throughout the year their food is predominantly vegetable, including the flowers, buds, leaves and seeds of low-growing plants, and cereal grains from stubble fields.

On heavy, sticky land chicks sometimes get hard balls of soil adhering to their feet; this hampers their development and means that they are an easy target for a predator.

The red-leg's main call – there are several – is a rather harsh, seemingly irritable 'chuk-chuk-chukar', from which the related chukar gets its name.

Although now well established in England red-legs are an introduced species – from France. The first successful introduction took place in Suffolk around 1770, after some failures during the previous century.

Special Considerations In some ways the red-leg seems to have more affinity with the pheasant than with the grey partridge. It is not difficult to rear and, if correctly acclimatized, it will not stray far from its release point. Reared birds can, therefore, provide sporting shooting in October and to some extent take the pressure off the grey partridge. Because the red-leg is an inveterate runner it is not a worthwhile quarry if walked-up over dogs; and, if driven in flat country without suitable belts or high hedges, the shooting can also be dull. In hilly or undulating terrain, however, it can be quite spectacular.

As we said in the previous section, compared with the grey partridges, a disproportionate number tend to get shot, largely because the red-leg usually comes over the Guns in small groups or as single birds rather than as a confusing whirring covey.

The species will hybridize with the chukar – of which some numbers have been released recently – but not with the grey partridge. The chukar is reared by some specialist game farms in this country – partly for the table and partly for release on shooting estates as a hybrid, after being crossed with the red-leg. The hybrid can be quite a good flyer in suitable surroundings, but chick survival is poor. The pure red-leg is to be preferred.

Red Grouse (*Lagopus lagopus scoticus*)

The red grouse – perhaps the most famous British gamebird – was once regarded as the only truly British species. Now, however, it is said to be a relation of the Scandinavian willow grouse, a bird which has white wings for most of the year but which turns completely white in winter. The red grouse can, nevertheless, still be considered unique in many respects. It is only found in the UK and attempts to introduce and establish it on heather moors in other European countries have so far failed.

Red grouse (Lagopus lagopus scoticus)

The nests are found usually in medium-short heather, fairly close to a path or edge of some kind and, in particular, the edge of a tract that has been burned; there are about eight mottled, reddish-brown eggs per clutch. The size of the clutch and the viability of the eggs and chicks are related to the nutrient quality of the heather eaten by the hen during the laying period. If it is growing well hatchability, stamina and so on will be good; if it has been dried or killed by harsh winds and frost it will be poor. Disease levels in the birds are also important to successful breeding.

Heather condition – and therefore grouse nutrition – is improved by burning strips or patches of the moor on a rotation every ten years or so; the rotation depending on local conditions. On some moors over-burning by accident and unbalanced grazing by sheep result in the replacement of the essential heather by rough grasses which are unpalatable to grouse. On well-managed moors with good quality heather containing a proportion of succulent young plants, grouse populations usually provide a surplus of young birds, allowing about 30–50 per cent to be harvested from 12 August onwards. Grouse is a valuable asset to the moors and earns the country foreign currency from visiting sportsmen.

Other important factors in grouse management include the draining of wet moors to encourage the heather to return; the provision of suitable grit so that the birds can grind up the heather in their gizzards; and control of predators – chiefly foxes and crows.

Male grouse are highly territorial and, unlike partridges, they defend the boundaries of their territory. The older birds take up territories first and the courting of females cannot occur until a territory has been established. The density of these territories varies from season to season and fluctuations in grouse numbers can be partly governed by cycles. Parasitic worms (*Trichostrongylus tenuis* – normally known as 'strongyles') are sometimes found in huge numbers in the intestines of red grouse. Recent research suggests that the numbers of worms can be, at times, high enough to affect grouse stocks and be responsible for the cyclic tendency of this species.

In some areas red grouse can sustain losses as a result of a tick-borne virus disease, known as louping-ill, which also affects sheep. Severe effects on chick survival have been reported and are now the subject of intensive research.

As with most gamebird species grouse have about fifteen to twenty different calls, the best known being a rapidly repeated and loud 'g'bek, g'bek'.

Special Considerations There are few, if any, special considerations to concern the grouse shooter. Basic moor management is fairly well understood, though it is not always possible to put it into practice. In a wet season, for instance, there are never enough days of suitable weather in which to get the heather-burning (or muirburn) completed and the habitat will then deteriorate. And depending on local grazing agreements there may be too great a concentration of sheep on the moors – or on parts of the moors – to achieve the most appropriate and economic balance of the two enterprises – sheep and grouse. Some areas are undergrazed. The need for predator control is accepted. As has been pointed out elsewhere in this book, driven grouse – with the butts at different levels up the hillside – can provide the most dangerous shooting of all. Only a careful appraisal of one's surroundings and the positions of the other Guns before each drive, combined with rigorous self-discipline, will ensure that accidents do not happen.

Black Grouse (*Lyrurus tetrix*)

The male is called a blackcock, the female a greyhen; together they are often referred to as blackgame. The cock, with its lyre-shaped tail, white wing-bar and glossy black plumage is easy to recognize; the cryptically coloured hen could possibly be confused by an inexperienced observer with a capercaillie hen, although the greyhen is much smaller. Blackgame will occasionally hybridize with capercaillie, red grouse and even pheasants, and such progeny are not always easy to identify.

In former times blackgame occurred in many localities in England and Wales as well as Scotland but, owing to habitat changes and possibly inconsiderate shooting, its range south of the border is now much more restricted. In most parts of Europe, where it takes a slightly different form, it is declining generally. In the UK there are hopes that population is at present more stable.

Its habitat includes the wooded fringes of moorland, rather than open moors, and the edges of woodland or scattered plantations. Some trees or shrubs appear to be an essential requirement provided they do not form a

Blackgame (Lyrurus tetrix)

R.M

dense stand. Like capercaillie, blackgame can cause damage to young forestry plantations. Blackgame are also to be found on upland farms; they are fond of oat crops, rushy meadows and old pastures. Dairy farms with silage crops in the vicinity do not favour the species.

The food of blackgame varies greatly according to the season but is predominantly vegetable; it includes heather, pine shoots, berries, catkins – especially of birch – buds, grasses, seeds, cereals and many other plant items. Young chicks will take insects such as ants and spiders.

Blackgame are promiscuous: there is no pair bond. The sexes only meet for copulation during extraordinary gatherings, called 'leks', which often take place in traditional places, 'arenas', about mid-March, continuing until mid-May. There is sometimes an autumn lek. Here the cocks go through ritual displays and 'dances' which are so unique that they have been frequently filmed and televised. The planting up of traditional arenas for leks or the disturbance of these areas can have a very adverse effect on blackgame.

Nests are made in heaths or scattered woods; six–ten eggs, pale, buff, lightly spotted with reddish-brown, are laid usually from early May onwards. The cock takes no part in nest building, incubation or caring for the brood.

Blackgame cannot be – or perhaps one should say are very rarely – managed properly like red grouse, nor are they as tractable to drive. When they do come over the Guns it should be remembered that, whereas grouse shooting begins on 12 August, *the blackgame season does not start until 20 August*; even then they are often not mature enough to shoot. Blackgame fly faster than grouse; they are also heavier – an adult cock weighing from 3lb8oz(1.58kg) to over 4lb(1.81kg) and a greyhen from 2lb4oz(1.02kg) to 3lb(1.36kg); a red grouse cock would be only about 1lb8oz(0.68kg) and the hen 1lb5oz(0.59kg).

Blackgame have a number of calls but the dove-like bubbling song, 'roo-kooing', which can carry a long way and is heard chiefly in the spring, is one of the most typical.

Special Considerations The blackgame population is almost everywhere in decline, though habitat deterioration and the invasion of the wilder places by more and more people are probably as much to blame as over-shooting. There are, however, some areas where increased afforestation of a suitable nature has resulted in their range being locally extended.

Today the average sporting estate owner is well aware of the situation and would normally advise his guests when it may or may not be appropriate to take a reasonable bag.

Capercaillie (*Tetrao urogallus*)

Capercaillie are now to be found only in Scotland, having perished south of the border and in Ireland some time around 1785, owing mostly to the clearance of the native pine forests. The poacher and the hunter probably accelerated the demise. At one time the species was also extinct in Scotland.

Many decades later, in 1837, during a period when the Scottish hillsides were being replanted with pines, a successful reintroduction of birds from Sweden took place on a Perthshire estate. Young were reared in captivity, released and additional eggs produced from captive stock were placed in wild greyhen nests – a technique that proved successful.

The caper – as it is often called – is the largest of all living British gamebirds, being about the size of a small turkey: the cock weighing up to 12lbs(5.44kg). The male is a handsome, dark bird, appearing almost black when glimpsed in the tops of pine trees, though at close quarters its plumage will be seen to be made up of dark greys, iridescent greens and browns flecked with white. In flight a large white area will be seen, particularly under its wing.

The hen is smaller with a background of mottled reddish-brown, barred with darker tones, and blending well with the woodland floor of heather and fallen pine needles where she nests. Capercaillie will hybridize with blackgame and occasionally with pheasants.

Their most favoured habitat consists of open, mature pine forest or mixed pine and broad-leaved woodlands, preferably with some glades or clearings where an undergrowth of heather and bilberry can be found. Aspen and rowan are also important. Capercaillie will sometimes damage seedling trees in forest nurseries, particularly if they are near plantations or groups of mature trees adopted by them, and from time to time foresters have regarded them as pests. In the winter and early spring the capercaillie's diet consists mainly of needles of the Scots pine. Later in the year bilberry, heather and a great variety of other vegetable foods are taken. The chicks feed on insects.

In April – normally in the very early morning – the cocks start displaying at small communal leks: to intimidate other cocks and to captivate the hens. The hens will only mate with a mature, dominant cock. It is at this time of the year that the curious metallic clicking call is emitted by the cocks. The onset of egg-laying varies according to the altitude and other local conditions, but is usually towards the end of April. The nest, lined with pine needles, is usually made at the base of an old

Capercaillie (Tetrao urogallus)

conifer, but sometimes in the heather on open moorland. The eggs have a pale reddish-buff background which is speckled and blotched with darker tones. The average clutch is about eight. When the range is being extended the hens colonize any new areas first.

In some countries the caper is regarded as big game and stalked with a .22 rifle. In Scotland, on those estates where there is a surplus of birds, they are driven like pheasants and can come over the Guns very fast and high.

Special Considerations Perhaps there are two lessons to be learned: firstly, that habitat deterioration can mean the end of a species. Secondly, that wise and imaginative conservation measures – in this case involving re-stocking – can bring about the recovery of a species. Good management can then ensure its stability.

Ptarmigan (*Lagopus mutus*)

Ptarmigan are probably the least-known members of the grouse family; they are only to be found at a high elevation in the wilder and more remote parts of the Scottish highlands. Their summer plumage, seen from above, provides the perfect camouflage amongst the heather and grasses, the mosses and lichen-covered rocks and boulders of those high and rather barren uplands. When flying it can be seen that the wing feathers and some of their under-parts are white. Their plumage varies greatly and undergoes a number of changes. In winter, like their cousins the willow grouse of Scandinavia, they turn almost entirely white to blend in with snowy backgrounds. They can sometimes be seen dusting or bathing in the snow, as well as digging into it for protection.

Mainly for ecological reasons red grouse and ptarmigan do not often occupy the same ground – their environmental requirements are somewhat different. The ptarmigan's typical habitat is not usually found below 2,500ft(760m), though much depends on the locality. Like the red

Ptarmigan (Lagopus mutus)

grouse ptarmigan are territorial and the cock defends his territory with a clear, rattling song, as well as threat calls. His more usual voice consists of a hoarse croak.

The food of ptarmigan includes heather shoots, also the shoots, flowers and berries of bilberry and crowberry – and many other items of the scant vegetation that is found at this altitude.

Pairing commences from the end of February onwards – depending on weather conditions – and copulation takes place towards the end of April. The ptarmigan is monogamous. Nesting usually begins early in May: the average clutch varying from five–eight eggs. The eggs are rather like those of the red grouse, but smaller, with a paler background and dark brown blotches. Nests are not infrequently robbed by gulls and crows. The main hatch takes place during the third week in June; the young are very precocious and capable of flying within two weeks of hatching.

Predators, which are especially troublesome during nesting, also include golden eagles and foxes, although the latter tend to be rather scarce at high altitudes.

The ptarmigan's range is thought to be slowly contracting; some of this is due to human intervention – probably indirect more than direct. In the Cairngorms the birds have adapted well to increased disturbance from skiing.

The ptarmigan weighs a little less than a red grouse. They are usually shot by walking-up with dogs.

Special Considerations None.

Woodcock (*Scolopax rusticola*)

The woodcock is widely distributed as a breeding bird in temperate regions of Europe and Asia as far east as Japan; in North America it is replaced by a smaller but otherwise similar species.

Although closely related to shore birds and officially a wader (and not legally game) the woodcock, as its name suggests, is found mainly in woodland. It is a solitary, retiring species – often going unnoticed due to its superbly camouflaged plumage and crepuscular habits. In southern Britain the preferred habitat for breeding is dry, secluded, broadleaved or mixed woodland, with frequent clearings and a light ground–cover of brambles and bracken. Clumps of evergreens, such as hollies or laurels, are appreciated. Wild rhododendron, scrub or even gorse, interspersed with rides or clearings, will also hold woodcock, provided the nearby feeding

Woodcock (Scolopax rusticola)

is adequate. In northern Britain birch woods are favoured and in many areas young forestry plantations are being increasingly utilized for breeding.

In winter woodcock spend the day in thicker cover, especially rhododendrons, holly or gorse, and at dusk they fly out to feed on pasture fields. In all seasons the diet is composed of earthworms and other soil-dwelling invertebrates, particularly insects and their larvae. Most food is obtained by probing in soft ground with the long, stout bill. This has a prehensile tip which enables worms to be seized as with forceps. For a long while it was believed that food was located solely by touch, but recent research indicates that smell may be involved as well. Prolonged spells with frozen ground, as in the 1981–82 winter, cause heavy mortality amongst woodcock and – with migrating northern populations from Scandinavia and west Russia augmenting the winter numbers in Britain – such hard weather may severely deplete breeding stocks in Britain and Europe.

The woodcock's breeding system is unusual in that the male woodcock is polygamous: one dominant bird may successively mate with several different females during a season. Some males will never acquire mates. Males do not defend an exclusive area to which females are attracted and in which nesting takes place. The onset of breeding is characterized by the strange display flight termed 'roding'. From February to July, at dusk and dawn, the male travels in ghostly fashion above the woodland canopy uttering at frequent intervals a series of curious croaks, followed immediately by a far-carrying squeak. After finding and mating with a female and staying with her until she starts to lay, the male cock will then go off in search of another.

The clutch of eggs – normally four – is laid in a small depression in the ground, lined only with dead leaves and invariably sited beneath a bramble stem or fallen branch. The female alone incubates, sitting motionless for long periods and relying on her camouflage for protection. Some do, however, fall victim to foxes. The eggs hatch after twenty-one days and the young fly when three weeks old. Unusually for a wader the young are probably fed by the parent for the first few days or so after hatching.

The female woodcock is credited with the ability to carry her young away from danger or to better feeding areas. The woodcock has several other unique features, one being its enormous eyes which enable it to see sufficiently well to move around at low-light intensities. Their positioning, high up on the head, also provides the bird with 360-degree vision, even when the bill is immersed. Accommodating these eye sockets has necessitated the rotation of the brain, so that the woodcock may truly be said to have an 'upside-down' brain. The pin feathers (vestigial first primaries) are highly prized by sportsmen and, in the past, were used by artists for fine work. Cock and hen woodcock cannot be told apart, except when held in the hand and examined closely by an expert.

Special Considerations In the UK the overall population – breeding and immigrant together – has remained fairly stable for a number of years and a careful watch is kept on the situation. We believe, however, that some European countries may be harvesting too many. Hunters cannot increase or replace the woodcock supply as they can with species such as pheasant and mallard.

Dangerous shots sometimes occur when woodcock shooting. Flushed on a pheasant day, this bird often seems to take a hunter by surprise; the inexperienced sportsman can get excited and take a wild shot.

Quail (*Coturnix coturnix*)

The quail, which is the smallest of our gamebirds, looks rather like a miniature partridge. It is the only British gamebird that migrates. From bill to tail it is no more than 7ins(178mm) long, whereas a cock partridge is a little over 12ins(305mm). A quail weighs 3–4oz(85–113g). Its ventriloquial call is supposed to resemble 'wet-my-lips'. It has rather secretive habits and, except on migration, does not take wing a great deal unless threatened, preferring to move about quietly in rough grasses, cornfields and other such vegetation which affords concealment. When it does fly it rises quickly and whirrs away for a relatively short distance before dropping down again.

Quail are widely distributed in Europe, North Africa and Western Asia. Its numbers in the UK fluctuate greatly and one speaks of 'quail years'. These occur partly because the UK is on the edge of its summer migration range and the effect of the weather can therefore be considerable. The birds usually arrive in May and most depart again in October. Groups of quail are termed 'bevies'.

The nest is usually made in growing corn, the clutch varying from seven–twelve: the colour of the eggs consists of a background of cream or pale tea, speckled or blotched with various shades of brown. Although the cock is attentive during incubation and the pair sing duets, only the hen sits on the eggs and looks after the brood when hatched. Being small and rather elusive, quail have not been studied in the same detail as partridges but it is assumed that they take much the same food.

In the Middle East migrating quail were at one time netted for the table in hundreds of thousands but this practice has now been reduced by international agreement. Quail served in British restaurants are the Japanese species which are reared in captivity like poultry.

Special Considerations The quail is fully protected in the UK and may not be shot. Nevertheless, we thought that a note on its habits should be included for the sake of completeness.

13
'Various'

A game-record book or a game register contains headings for all the more common species such as pheasants, partridges, grouse and other well-known quarry. Some also have separate columns for what might be described as lesser quarry, typified by woodpigeons, hares and rabbits. The remaining species that are not listed separately are grouped together under 'Various'. Here the Gun can record any other species shot during the day, including pests such as jays, magpies, grey squirrels and so on.

There is no place in this book for descriptions and life histories of all these 'various' birds and beasts that may legitimately be shot. But the young sportsman would be wise to study them just as carefully as the more important quarry. For example, there is a difference between a rook and a crow: the man with a gun should be familiar with it. A long-tailed furry creature leaping half-hidden through the leafy branches might be a grey *or* a red squirrel. Be quite certain before you shoot! The latter is now very rare in places and, to some extent, protected.

In all cases a good maxim is, 'When in doubt do *not* shoot!' It also seems senseless to shoot species that you do not intend to eat – other than pests.

Hare

Brown Hare (*Lepus capensis*[1])

The Brown hare has a very wide geographical range, being found not only in Britain but right across Europe and as far as southern Africa. It is an

---

1. Until fairly recently known as *Lepus europaeus*.

animal of the open country and plains and, in Britain, has become adapted to the arable farmland landscape. It will also frequent woodlands. Some differences between the hare and the rabbit are described in the next section, 'Rabbit'.

Hares and rabbits have a completely vegetable diet; the hare feeds primarily on weeds, grasses and cereals in their early stages – only in conditions of food shortage are they forced to damage and bark young tree saplings. This can often happen in the winter when their preferred foods are covered with snow and ice. The animals feed at night. Digestion takes place in two phases: during the day large soft pellets from the caecum, or cavity where the large intestine begins, pass down the gut and out through the anus, and are immediately eaten again by the hare. These soft pellets are then digested a second time and pass straight through, being deposited at night as the familiar round pellets or droppings. This strange process of eating their faeces (known as 'refection') provides a very efficient way of breaking down the cellulose material in vegetation.

Hares are comparatively large animals: the male weighs on average $7\frac{1}{2}$lbs(3.5kg) and the females are slightly heavier at 8lbs(3.7kg). Outwardly the two sexes look very similar and generally it is not possible to tell them apart unless they are extremely close. The coat is mostly brownish-tan in colour, a little brighter than the more subdued greyish-brown of the rabbit. Very occasionally hares may live up to twelve years in suitable conditions, but normally on farmland four years is about the maximum age. Indeed, where hares are shot, the hare population turns over fairly quickly, with about 35 per cent of the stock being less than a year old in autumn. The hare breeding season is very extended and it is possible to see young leverets in almost every month of the year, but normally breeding starts in February and finishes during October. Most hares are probably born in the early summer months. Females produce three or four litters a year, with two to three leverets in each litter.

Little is really known of the hare's behaviour, but recent work suggests that it is not a solitary animal as once supposed, but commonly found in groups; and in spring it is common to see hares sitting close to each other in pairs. The 'March madness' often seen in hares appears to be the result of breeding behaviour, where a male will closely follow a female and the characteristic chasing and running in circles develops. The 'boxing' displays are probably not fights between rival males, but more likely females fending off the attentions of over-zealous males. The young leverets are born fully furred with their eyes fully open and, within a few days, the female will move them to separate dugout forms within her normal home-range. The young are normally nursed for only five minutes every twenty-four hours just after dusk, and it is at this time of day that leverets are most commonly seen when they come out and follow their mother.

There appears to have been a steady reduction in hare numbers on most of Britain's farmland during the last twenty years – although they are still most abundant in the arable parts of Britain, especially where a high proportion of cereals are grown. The causes for this decline in hare numbers are not yet determined, but it appears to have been widespread in most of Western Europe. The intensification of agriculture and particularly the increased use of pesticides are widely blamed although, at the moment, there is little concrete evidence to demonstrate that this is the case. The increase in the fox population and the effect of early autumn cultivations, when their cover vanishes rapidly and leaves the ground very bare, are almost certainly part of the reason why hares are declining.

A farmer's hare shoot

In view of the present decline sportsmen would be advised to make quite sure that over-shooting does not take place. As stated, in certain areas hares are now at a very low density; in other places – like rabbits – they are still too numerous for farming interests and can do damage to crops, especially roots and crops grown by market gardeners. Often such damage is done by one or two individual animals, which can be culled quite easily.

Where hares are plentiful special drives are organized in open country – taking in fairly large sweeps of farmland. These drives usually take place in the winter months towards the end of, or after, the pheasant shooting.

The line of beaters always contains walking Guns and this form of shooting can be dangerous, unless great care is taken. It is usual to invite farmers and others to come out on such days, many of whom only shoot a gun once or twice a year. They tend to forget the basic safety rules and will swing through the line and not take into account ricochets off flints and other stones. The novice should always remember *never* to take a long shot at a hare: a wounded squealing hare draws most unwelcome attention to the person who took the shot.

Hares are also a part of the rough-shooter's quarry, as anyone who has had to carry a couple of them in his game bag for an hour or so will know! They are also commonly seen on pheasant and partridge days where their numbers are still reasonably high. Some shoots do not like them killed in the warm weather and the organizers will say so.

Blue Hare (*Lepus timidus*)

In mountainous regions in Britain the brown hare is replaced by the mountain or blue hare. It is a rather smaller animal which prefers a moorland and alpine environment to farmland. It occurs in Scotland, Wales and the Peak District, usually above the levels of cultivation. It does not make a 'form' like the brown hare but hides among stone, tussocks of rough grass, heather or rushes. It is not so good to eat as the brown hare and is normally shot incidentally when one is out after game on the moors or in the hills. In the winter its coat turns almost entirely white, except for the tips of the ears, which provides good camouflage in the snow.

Rabbit (*Oryctolagus cuniculus*)

The rabbit, unlike the mountain hare and brown hare, is not a native of Britain; it was introduced probably by the Normans for its value as meat and fur. It was, and still is, sometimes called a coney – the term used in the Authorized version of the Bible. During the Middle Ages, and until the eighteenth century, there were very few truly wild rabbits; most were in enclosed warrens where they were protected from predators and exploited commercially. Although numbers of rabbits escaped from these warrens it is unlikely they survived in the wild. By the eighteenth century, however, there was a large change in the rabbit population; the enclosed warrens became increasingly uncompetitive due to skins being imported from the New World. By 1900 the enclosed rabbit warren was a thing of the past.

Other events during the nineteenth century – particularly the great reduction of many predators and the large improvements in agricultural land – meant that rabbits were able to survive outside their enclosed warrens; from the 1850s onwards the wild-rabbit population began to build up rapidly to damaging proportions. In 1954 it was legally defined as a pest. In 1974 the National Farmers Union estimated that rabbits were consuming some £100 million worth of farm crops annually.

The increase in rabbit numbers was only halted by the advent of myxomatosis in 1954 which killed more than 99 per cent of the wild population. Since then, rabbit numbers have been steadily increasing, although they are not as yet back at the pre-myxomatosis level. The virus is transmitted from one rabbit to another, principally by the flea in Britain; in other countries, such as Australia, the mosquito is the most important carrier. The disease is still to be found in rabbit populations in this country, a major outbreak usually occurring regularly between August and December. It is now far less virulent than when it first appeared and a greater proportion of the animals now suffer only a minor attack from which they recover, giving the individual rabbits immunity for the rest of their lives. Some rabbit populations have developed a considerable degree of genetic resistance to the disease.

Rabbits are prolific breeders (January to August) and females can produce four–six litters annually, the number of young varying from three to eight. They are not promiscuous as was once thought, but polygamous – one buck keeping company with several does, each of which has her own territory within a warren. The young are born in a short tunnel or stop in the warren and at birth are deaf, blind and without fur; at about ten days the eyes and ears open. From about three weeks they start making short journeys from the nest. They are suckled once in about twenty-four hours and weaned at a month, though they will start taking solid food at the sixteenth day. Young rabbits can breed at three–four months.

Rabbits are mainly nocturnal feeders like the hare, though sportsmen will also commonly see them feeding at dawn and dusk; in undisturbed places they may continue to feed during the day. Heavy rain, strong winds and snow will drive them down into their burrows. Rabbits are also like hares in that all food eaten is passed through their gut twice.

In appearance they are different: rabbits are smaller than hares, weighing 3–4lbs(1.2–2kg). They also have relatively shorter legs and ears than hares. Their fur is mostly greyish except for slightly sandy colouring at the nape of the neck. The absence of the black tip to the ears is an important distinguishing feature from hares: also the tail looks like a small powder puff and is held erect against the body when running.

Ferreting

Ferrets have been used to bolt rabbits from their burrows since Roman times. The ferret itself is a member of the weasel family and exhibits the same characteristics of fearlessness and agility. The polecat is virtually the same creature in the wild state and the white ferret with its pink eyes is the albino form. White ferrets are particularly useful when working in undergrowth because they stand out sharply and can be seen more easily by the handler. Small ferrets can be used to bolt rats, while stoats and even cats and foxes have been evicted!

Handling from an early age, at eight weeks, is essential to bring up a placid, friendly ferret that will emerge freely from the earth after rabbits or rats have bolted. An experienced sportsman will know to approach a ferret slowly and carefully, and to pick it up so that the animal feels at ease. Even the quietest ferret is capable of inflicting a sharp, painful nip on anyone who frightens or mishandles it.

The best time of the year for ferreting rabbits is from November to March when there is less likelihood of young being resident. Bright frosty mornings tend to produce better sport than warm, wet conditions.

Ordinary working ferrets seem to thrive better in company so it is advisable to start by acquiring two of the same sex. Jills (females) come into season twice a year and sometimes die prematurely if allowed to pass their second heat without mating. A 'liner' may also be kept. His job is to drag a line or nowadays more commonly carry a small radio transmitter (or bleeper) down to a kill and then behave sufficiently unsociably to persuade other ferrets to leave and return to the surface! He will remain with the kill – and act as a marker-buoy – until dug out. A large strong hob (male) is usually chosen for this duty and should be housed separately.

A well-ventilated carrying-box lined with straw, or a suitable sack, will

A ferret handler and his equipment

be required to transport the ferrets. A spade should be taken in case a kill is made and, even when shooting, a few purse-nets should be included and used where two or more holes are close together. Rabbits are otherwise inclined to run from hole to hole rather than bolt clear of the warren.

One man in the shooting party should be in charge of the ferrets and the remainder should take up shooting positions well clear of the burrow or 'bury'. The safe lines of fire should be clearly established by each Gun before a ferret is entered. *It is vital that the Guns know each other's positions and that of the handler.*

It is possible to use a steady dog to fetch shot rabbits, provided it has been trained not to retrieve or molest ferrets.

A major factor in successful ferreting operations is quietness when approaching and working around the warren. A lot of noise and disturbance above ground makes rabbits loath to bolt. This may be why purse-netting sometimes gives better results than shooting. Also netted rabbits fetch a better price than shot rabbits. To avoid excessive noise any holes overgrown with thorns or undergrowth should be cleared a few days before ferreting.

It is important to allow rabbits to bolt well away from the warren before shooting. Over-eager, trigger-happy Guns have been known to shoot the ferret. Furthermore, a rabbit wounded close to its burrow may be able to crawl back and this will necessitate a long dig to retrieve it. Further, rabbits shot at close range are of little use for human consumption, so it pays to let them run 15 or 20 yards before firing.

Normal 12-bore game cartridges are satisfactory for rabbit shooting over ferrets; an ounce load of No. 6 shot is quite sufficient. Some prefer to use a lighter gun: 20- or 28-bores are excellent weapons, but a .410 may be slightly under-powered once a rabbit is more than 15 yards away.

On a full day some milk should be provided for the ferrets at lunchtime, as they work hard. There are varying opinions as to how well-fed the ferret should be before work commences. At the end of the day a liver from the paunched rabbits, given to each ferret, should keep the little hunters satisfied and quiet on the journey home.

Ferrets should not be treated as 'poor relations' compared with trained gundogs. They must be properly fed and live in comfortable, hygienic conditions (see Short Bibliography) and a veterinary surgeon should be consulted if they become ill.

Stalking with a .22 Rifle

Many a youngster has progressed from shooting sparrows and starlings with an air gun to bigger game in the form of the rabbit. While some of the standard high-powered air rifles are sufficient to kill rabbits if a vital organ is hit, a 'pump-up' air rifle or a conventional .22 rifle are more suitable weapons; see chapter ten, 'The .22 Rifle'. Both require a Firearm Certificate.

Most rifles can be fitted with a silencer which commonly screws onto the muzzle. When using low-velocity (subsonic) ammunition for short-range targets the noise of firing is reduced to a dull 'phut'. With high-velocity rounds there is still a sharp crack, even when a silencer is employed.

Hollow-nosed or hollow-point (expanding) bullets should be used for all live targets as they have a much greater stopping power. Solid rounds can pass through an animal, which may then run several yards to its burrow although fatally wounded.

Next to humane considerations, the most important aspect of sporting rifle shooting is safety, discussed in so far as shotgun users are concerned in chapter seven, 'Safety and Security'. It is imperative to know where the shot will go, if it misses. Where possible the stalker should be on high ground and shoot into banks. Even in this situation there is danger from ricochets on flinty ground or in areas of hard rock. Silhouette shots should *never* be taken as one cannot know who or what may be over the sky-line, or hidden in the long grass.

The stalker will usually have his greatest success around dawn and dusk, the main feeding times for rabbits. On warm, dry, summer days rabbits may be out feeding at any time.

Most shots will probably be taken at less than 70yds(64m) and the rifle should be zeroed accordingly with the ammunition to be used. The two most killing areas for a rabbit are in the neck at reasonably close range, or in the heart (situated where the foreleg meets the body) for a longer shot. One should avoid aiming hopefully at the centre of a hunched rabbit as this can wound the animal in the stomach; it may still be able to run to a

Tempting targets for the .22 rifle shot, provided the angle of fire is at all times safe

nearby burrow. It will then, of course, die quite quickly, but the hunter likes to be sure of his shot and also to retrieve his quarry.

As in rook shooting, a stick can be helpful to steady the rifle, especially when shooting from a sitting, kneeling or standing position. A sling, used correctly, will also help.

It is a common fault to be over-hasty when encountering a large group of rabbits and try to get off a quick shot without aiming carefully and deliberately. Rabbits do not always panic and run when one of their number drops dead. But if they hear the thud of a bullet in the ground or see the earth fly up, this is almost certain to cause alarm.

Naturally all the aspects of fieldcraft will greatly affect the sportsman's bag: silence, as well as slow and cautious movement, is imperative. The wind should always be taken into account before setting forth.

Woodpigeon

There are five wild pigeon and dove species in Britain. The commonest one is the woodpigeon (*Columba palumbus*), sometimes called the ring-dove, cushat or quist.

There is also the stock-dove or blue rock – a little smaller and more compact than the 'woodie' and without any white on wings or neck. The rock-dove (because of its name, sometimes confused with the blue rock) is, in its pure form, now rare and local. Its main distinguishing characteristics are the two black wing-bars and the white rump. Our common urban or feral pigeons often show these black wing-bars and are domesticated strains of the rock-dove.

The turtle dove is much smaller than the first three, as is the newest arrival (breeding here since 1955), the collared dove, now assuming pest proportions.

The woodpigeon, though a handsome bird and a sporting quarry, cannot be said to be the farmer's friend. Its diet is varied and it is capable of causing considerable damage to many agricultural crops, including cereals, brassicas and legumes, although this tends to be regional.

An increase in woodpigeon numbers came about during the First World War when the farming landscape was radically changed. Cereal production was enormously increased and a great deal of land went under the plough for the first time. Cattle and sheep numbers increased, together with the food to feed them and the requisite waterpoints. Secondary growth left by intensive cutting of mature woodlands produced the perfect habitat for pigeons, as did the increased planting of

WOOD
PIGEON

ROCK DOVE

STOCK DOVE

TURTLE DOVE

COLLARED TURTLE DOVE

Pigeons and doves

mixed hardwoods and conifers. Recently, new crops like oil-seed rape have helped to provide the pigeon with food all the year round.

Pigeon numbers perhaps reached their peak in the 1950s; then came the hard winter of 1962–63 and many died of starvation. In due course the population recovered and remained fairly high until about 1968. From then on there was a decline; more recently there has been another gradual increase, although numbers have not yet returned to the level of the mid-1960s. Fluctuations in woodpigeon numbers are related to the changes in food supply brought about by differing agricultural practices.

Shooting pressure has also been very heavy – perhaps in some areas too heavy. The woodpigeon has for a long time been the main sport of shooting people in the lower-income groups: farm workers, rough-shooting clubs and others. Furthermore, until recent EEC regulations, there was a profitable export market for shot pigeons. The situation of possible over-shooting is one to be watched by the experts.

In certain areas, however, the woodpigeon is still present in sufficient numbers to cause harmful crop losses. There is really only one way to protect the farmer's crops from pigeons and that is to shoot them from a hide with the aid of decoys, on the field where they are doing damage. This applies to any crop at all times of the year. Carbide guns or other 'bangers' only keep pigeons off until they get used to them.

Although woodpigeons are not protected by law and there is no close season for them, one cannot simply go out and shoot them on somebody else's land. It is necessary to ask the owner, keeper, tenant farmer, agent, or whoever is responsible, for permission to go on the ground. Nowadays, with pigeon shooting so much in demand it is not so easy to get such permission. Such shooting is usually reserved for those who work on the farm or estate or who help in some such capacity as beaters.

Decoying Pigeon decoying is based on the fact that both the woodpigeon and the stock-dove are gregarious birds and like to feed in company. If, therefore, the Gun produces a decoy picture that looks like the real thing, a passing woodpigeon will readily join what he believes to be a group of feeding birds.

It is essential to know the pigeons' yearly diet sheet – what they are likely to eat each month. The shooter then begins to know where to go. Two types of reconnaissance are necessary: to identify the fields which the pigeons are using as a feeding area and to watch that field carefully in order to find out exactly where to site the hide. This may be made of straw bales, camouflage nets or cut brambles in a hedge.

A quickly made pigeon hide on the edge of a field.
(Photograph kindly donated by John Marchington)

A woodpigeon, as seen from a hide, landing amongst stuffed decoys.
(Photograph kindly donated by John Marchington)

The best place for the hide is usually under what might be called the 'pigeon traffic'; this may not necessarily be right for the wind. The Gun can then build his hide in the right place, preferably so as to face the pigeons coming in to land. Hide building is an art and cannot be described in one paragraph, but one or two points may be useful. When building a hide the shooter should always endeavour to construct a higher background, so that when he gets up to fire he is not so easily seen in stark silhouette. All hides should be made so that the Gun can sit down and look *through* the cover and not over the top. The Gun should not settle down in his hide until he has first walked or driven the pigeons right off the field.

Pigeon-shooting equipment is simple. A four-gallon oil-drum makes a good steady seat, a bill-hook is useful for cutting branches, and some old sacks to hold the dead birds complete the essentials.

The best decoy is a dead pigeon, set up realistically as though feeding, or a group of shot birds similarly arranged. If rubber or plastic decoys are used they can easily be dulled down or covered with real pigeon feathers to prevent 'shine'. One should start with at least ten and put them out at least 3–4 metres apart.

Now let the pigeons approach the decoys and shoot them when they are over them at the appropriate killing range. (The experts normally use Nos. 6 or 7 shot.) Use any lulls in the shooting to build up your decoy picture, that is, put out more dead birds and keep on doing so. Do not leave any birds on their backs, looking unnatural; collect up wounded birds immediately (though never allow a dog to hunt hedgerows in the game-nesting season). When you stop shooting tidy up everything as carefully as possible. Do not, for example, leave cartridge cartons and empty cases everywhere. If you have to pick up a towered bird some distance away, never leave your gun *loaded* in a hide. Also make certain that you always have a safe place against which to lean it. Do not forget that leaves, bits of twig, straw, etc., can get lodged in the barrel, so check this regularly. In a netting hide make sure the gun cannot be caught up in the net.

Never fire a low shot down or through a hedge unless you can clearly see that there is absolutely no danger. Watch out for farm workers and never fire anywhere near them.

Pigeon Flighting at Roost In addition to decoying there is another way of killing pigeons; this is to shoot them when they are coming back to the woods to roost – usually in the later winter. Whereas your decoying will be done during the day – and at dawn if it is very hot – roost shooting can only be carried out during the last hour or so of daylight.

The procedure is as follows. Having obtained permission to shoot a known roosting wood, search it carefully for the main 'droppings' area. Place yourself 40 yards up-wind of this area, sit with your back to a tree or other background, and watch. Do not make a hide until your observations tell you which direction the flight is taking. This will be your best place to intercept the flighting birds.

If you are carefully dressed to blend in with your surroundings – and you remember not to show a white face at the wrong moment – a hide may not be necessary, though a couple of branches bent over may help your camouflage.

Roost shooting is at its most productive when several Guns go out together, to keep the birds on the move from one wood to another over a fairly large area.

Do not shoot too late; *this allows pheasants to go up to roost in peace* and also permits pigeons to settle down so that you will get another chance to shoot in a week or two's time.

Rook and Crow

Rook (*Corvus frugilegus*)

Although there has been some local decline of the rook population, in many parts of Britain the species is still numerous enough to be of concern to gamekeepers and even wildlife-reserve wardens. Like all corvids they are expert egg thieves and they also kill young chicks. To their credit they eat grubs that are injurious to farm crops; the rook is virtually omnivorous.

One of the traditional ways of keeping rooks under control is to shoot the young 'branchers' with a .22 rifle just before they can fly. The date will vary from season to season but will usually be around the middle of May. If too much leaf is out the task can be difficult, for the nests and young rooks will be largely hidden from view.

On a calm day with the branches still reasonably bare and in a rookery of only medium height, sport will not be unduly difficult: the shooting merely becomes a pest-control exercise. Nevertheless, it can be of great value to game managers. In a high tree with a strong wind blowing, however, a young rook perching on the edge of a swaying nest can provide a very testing target.

For humanitarian reasons the shooter should use only .22 hollow-point, rather than solid, ammunition. If a bird should be winged and fall back into the nest the shooter must wait until the bird shows itself again or put one or two heavy shotgun charges into the nest. In a rook-shooting party it is often the custom for one member of the team to bring a shotgun to deal with any young rooks that may be more advanced than the others and take wing at the first crack of the rifle.

Before tackling the rookeries all weapons should be zeroed as for target shooting. To keep the rifle steady a sling can be used or advantage taken of any nearby tree trunk or gatepost. A stout stick – as used in roe stalking – may also help.

As explained elsewhere, permission to shoot rookeries must always be obtained from the landowner concerned and safety precautions strictly observed.

Rook pie (using only the breasts of the young birds) sounds delicious in the recipe book but, unless there is a good deal more bacon, egg, pastry and seasoning than rook meat, the consumer may be disappointed!

Crow (*Corvus corone corone*)

Crows are even more serious destroyers of eggs and chicks than rooks but, as they are solitary nesters, different tactics such as flighting, or intercepting the quarry between two points, have to be employed. Gamekeepers will sometimes welcome assistance from good amateur shots.

Grey Squirrel (*Sciurus carolinensis*)

The grey squirrel, which is a native of the north-eastern United States and south-eastern Canada, has replaced the native red squirrel over large parts of England and central Scotland and is regarded as a very serious forest pest. Many trees are killed by the squirrels removing the bark, many more have the timber ruined or lose their tops when the damage is in the crown. Beech and sycamore are the species worst affected, but many others, including conifers, are attacked. Grey squirrels also eat nuts, bulbs and seeds, including peas, beans, maize and wheat, ripe and unripe fruit, and occasionally the eggs and young of songbirds and gamebirds. They love to raid bins and hoppers where food is put down for gamebirds and in this way can cost the pheasant shoot a great deal of money. They do not hibernate and may be seen searching for food at all times of the year.

Red squirrels still exist in some localities and can also damage trees. In most places, however, they are in decline: *they are now protected*, though if damage is being caused permission can be sought for local control.

Grey squirrels prefer mixed woodlands but are also encountered in pure conifer woods, especially when these are not very large. In the autumn, particularly, they may be found on the ground in hedgerows, gardens and fields and the young travel widely in the early summer, usually following the hedges. They are agile, cunning and inquisitive, have sharp hearing, some sense of smell and are normally shy of man. Grey squirrels live in hollow trees or in nests called 'dreys' constructed in tree tops.

Squirrels are most active in the early morning and evening. They can be stalked on the ground or in the trees and shot, either with a shotgun or, having due regard to safety, with a .22 rifle. No. 6 shot should be used to give a fairly dense pattern. For the rifle hollow-point ammunition – either standard or high velocity – should be used. A good telescopic sight (about four-power) with a fine cross-wire graticule is ideal.

Another good way to shoot squirrels in woods is for two Guns to work together, with a dog for marking. Dogs are attracted by squirrel scent and soon learn to mark a squirrel in the trees. When a squirrel 'freezes' it can be difficult for one man to shoot, as it moves its position with the shooter to keep hidden behind a branch or the tree trunk. When two Guns are present one should stand still while the other circles round the tree. When shooting alone it is a good tip to hang a coat on a bush – there is a good chance that the squirrel will watch the dummy and so lay itself open to the shooter. A squirrel that has 'frozen' will soon lose patience; the Gun should remain still for a few minutes and the squirrel will probably move.

A wounded squirrel should not be handled as it will bite viciously. It should be dispatched humanely with a sharp blow on the head or with a second shot.

Drey poking During the winter and early spring, on a cold and wet day, many squirrels will remain in their winter dreys. These are more compact than those made for summer occupation and often look like a leafy football. Squirrel poles are made of aluminium in short sections for transport. A useful squirrel hunting-team consists of three or more people; one with the drey-poking pole, one or two with shotguns for moving squirrels and a rifleman for the occasional static shot. Some dreys can be as high as 60 feet and poking is hard work, so it is fair to exchange roles from time to time. Sometimes several squirrels will leave the drey at once and the Guns need to be ready. *Great caution should, of course, be used in operating the metal pole anywhere near electricity lines.* Squirrels need not be thrown away. Their meat is quite good eating – considered a delicacy in the United States – and the tails are in demand for tying trout flies.

14
Wildfowling Today

For many centuries duck, goose and wader shooting has been part of life on estuaries around our coast. The participant was, and still is, referred to as a 'wildfowler' and he continues to follow old traditions established by professional wildfowlers – although the sport is now restricted to certain edible quarry species only. Normally the wildfowler is on foot but, in some circumstances, boats are used. A thoroughly modern recreation, it rewards the correct use of ancient skills as well as an understanding of nature. It requires toughness and perseverance. It can provide comradeship and a source of food.

Purists will argue that true wildfowling is strictly a coastal activity, taking place below the high-water mark, that is, on the foreshore around the coast. Duck and goose flighting, however, does take place inland on marshes, lakes and specifically managed flight ponds. Many mallard are reared, released and shot on shoots throughout the country.

The rational use of a renewable resource does not presuppose the latter's eventual depletion. All healthy animal and bird populations produce a surplus of individuals each year. Proper exploitation of such a resource by wildfowling ensures that no more than the surplus of a wildfowl population is removed; the well-being of that population is thereby assured.

There is very little free wildfowling in Britain nowadays since shooting rights are almost always held by landowners or shooting tenants under a measure of control defined by the Game Act 1831, Game (Scotland) Act 1832 and the Firearms Act 1968. In England and Wales the traditional place for wildfowling is that part of the seashore which is more often than not covered by the flux and reflux of the four ordinary tides occurring midway between springs and neaps. This is called the foreshore and much of it is in Crown ownership or subject to control by the holders of regulating leases from the Crown Estate Commissioners. The remaining parts are in private hands. In England and Wales the British Association for Shooting and Conservation (formerly WAGBI) has an agreement with the Crown Estate Commissioners and with the Duchy of Lancaster, whereby its members will not be prosecuted for carrying shotguns on the foreshore controlled by the Crown or the Duchy. Elsewhere, it must be stressed, permission is required to shoot on private foreshores; the onus is on the wildfowler to establish whether the foreshore is private. Access and egress must be by public right of way unless otherwise authorized in writing. The only rights for members of the public on English and Welsh foreshores are those of fishing and navigation.

In Scotland the foreshore is defined slightly differently as the area between high- and low-water marks of ordinary spring tides. In Scotland, whether the ownership pertains to the Crown or to a private individual, the Crown retains in trust for the public certain rights including recreation on the foreshore (except in Orkney and the Shetlands), by virtue of which members of the public may engage in wildfowling. This public right may only be taken away by statute, as by the establishment of nature reserves under the National Parks and Access to the Countryside Act 1949, by declaration of sanctuaries under the Wildlife and Countryside Act 1981, or the establishment of country parks under the Countryside (Scotland) Act 1967. As before, the onus is on the wildfowler to establish whether such statutory controls exist.

Understanding the Habits of Your Quarry

Ducks In broad terms ducks feed by night, flighting between feeding and resting places at dawn and dusk. On the foreshore ducks will also feed in daylight and their habits will be affected by the tide. The stronger the tide and the rougher the water, the more marked will be the movement of birds.

Geese Geese feed by day, flighting between the feeding and resting places at dawn and dusk. On moonlit nights, however, some species, in particular pink-footed and white-fronted geese, will flight back to their feeding grounds from their roost. The roost may be a large expanse of inland water or on the open shore or sea. During the few nights around full moon they may even remain on the feeding grounds throughout the whole period.

Waders Movement of wading birds is largely based on the tides as they feed almost exclusively in the intertidal zone. Curlew and golden plover are the only quarry waders which regularly flight inland and feed on pastures; but only curlew join the strictly tidal quarry waders such as redshank, grey plover and bar-tailed godwits on their night roost. Some waders which were once wildfowlers' quarry are now protected; see page 124 under 'Waders'.

Coastal Shooting

Coastal shooting provides immense variety. When high winds and rough weather prevail, tide flighting or decoying wigeon on the flashes which remain after the tide has ebbed can provide some of the season's most exciting sport. Wigeon flight well under the moon too.

Successful wildfowlers rarely achieve satisfactory bags without acquiring a detailed knowledge of local conditions. This includes information about the prevailing and expected weather, the tides, and their combined effect on flighting and feeding of the birds. Observation of such matters can be every bit as fascinating as the actual shooting. Binoculars are an essential piece of equipment.

At the beginning of the season, which starts on 1 September, the foreshore shooter will expect to see wildfowl and waders which have bred in Britain. At dawn and dusk mallard and teal establish flight lines to and from their inland feeding grounds. At this time, as many mallard will be feeding on corn stubbles, the wildfowler will endeavour to place himself strategically where he can intercept their flight.

During these early weeks of the season the birds, such as barley-fed mallard, are at their best for eating. By October the migratory duck and geese will have started to arrive in large numbers. Most estuaries are visited by small parties of migratory mallard, wigeon, teal and pintail, to supplement the resident populations of mallard and teal.

Once wintry weather prevails, the wildfowler is in his element; the best results are often achieved when conditions are at their worst. Strong winds, in particular, keep the wildfowl on the move in an effort to find

The late Dr Jeffery Harrison and his labradors on the Medway

shelter; when the freshwater inland marshes freeze up wildfowl are forced to move to the more open coastal areas.

Under prolonged and extreme wintry weather hungry birds rapidly lose body condition and become tame and approachable – thus no longer a worthy quarry. At such time the true sportsman has no need to be told when to use restraint, but the Wildlife and Countryside Act 1981 empowers the Secretary of State to invoke a statutory ban on wildfowling until the conditions have improved and the birds have recovered their health.

Inland Shooting

Low-lying areas in the vicinity of estuaries can provide excellent sport for the inland duck shooter. Water meadows, dykes, channels and flashes will attract wildfowl and it is to such areas that the duck flight at dusk, attracted by easy feeding conditions. Not all birds will flight back to the coast to rest during the day; some of the large expanses of water inland provide good day roosting areas, particularly when conditions on the coast are rough and inhospitable. They are also used extensively by pochard and tufted duck as roosting and feeding sites.

Many estates in Britain have sheltered lakes which are used as resting areas and where duck shooting will take place. Such areas are normally flighted at dawn with care being taken not to shoot too frequently. Decoys can sometimes be used successfully to concentrate the duck near the hides.

Planning Your Sport

When you go out on a stretch of foreshore for the first time, it is prudent to go in daylight with someone who knows the area and can point out marsh boundaries and any dangers which may exist locally. When wildfowling away from home it is usual to make contact with the local wildfowling club secretary to ensure that you do not inadvertently encroach on private ground. Make sure you know the local rules and restrictions, particularly if operating in, or near, a nature reserve shooting area.

Always tell someone where you propose to go wildfowling and also tell him or her that you have returned safely.

Always consult the tide tables before going on the shore and remember that the tide-height figures stated will be altered by the prevailing weather conditions. If British Summer Time is in force remember to make the necessary correction to your tide table. Avoid the more distant parts of the shore when a big tide is expected.

Wear comfortable, inconspicuous, warm, waterproof clothing that will not restrict movement too much. A large canvas bag is useful and can be used to sit on. Thigh boots or waders are normally recommended.

Equipment Essentials include a pocket compass to enable you to get back safely on a previously noted bearing; a waterproof wristwatch for judging the state of the tide; a good torch and whistle which can be used for signalling in an emergency. A further safety precaution would be a hand-held flare of the type used in sea-rescue operations. A pair of lightweight binoculars is essential for quarry identification and on certain marshes a six-foot wading pole will help when walking on soft ground; it can also be used to sound dykes and crossing places before wading out. Always carry a pull-through (it is easy to get mud in the muzzle of a gun).

Every wildfowler should have a reliable dog, trained for the water

A strong, water-loving, retrieving dog should always be taken along when wildfowling.

Guns and Cartridges[1]

A double-barrelled 12-bore is a suitable all-round shotgun and the standard game load of $2\frac{1}{2}$ins(64mm) cartridge will cope with most shots. Modern guns are chambered for $2\frac{3}{4}$ins(70mm) heavy-load cartridges which will give slightly greater range; the skilled wildfowler, however, will get sufficiently close to his quarry before shooting.

Big-bore guns, such as 10-, 8- and 4-bores, although capable of firing heavier loads more effectively, tend to be cumbersome and nowadays less popular.

Rifles must not be used for wildfowling; semi-automatic shotguns should be fitted with a device to prevent the firing of more than three cartridges in succession without reloading. For shot sizes most suitable for various species see the following table (repeated from page 54).

1. See also chapter eight, 'Sporting Guns and Cartridges'.

Shot Sizes for Various Quarries

Duck	4, 5 or 6
Geese	BB, 1 or 3
Grouse, partridge, teal, woodcock, waders	6 or 7
Hare	4 or 5
Pheasant	5, 6 or 7
Pigeon	6 or 7
Rabbit	5 or 6
Snipe	7 or 8

A wide range of waterproof cartridges is available and these are particularly recommended for wildfowl shooting.

Behaviour on the Marsh[1]

When arriving on the foreshore or marsh early in the morning or when leaving late at night, do not spoil the sport for any other wildfowler by banging car doors or making any undue noise. Do not arrive late or depart early, thereby disturbing the shooting of others who have taken the trouble to get into position in good time. Never shoot in the immediate vicinity of houses.

Make sure you are well hidden and camouflaged to suit your surroundings.

Keep well clear of other shooters on the foreshore. Do not shoot at anything which may endanger another person within range.

Try to make your dog comfortable – if you sit on your game bag, try to ensure he also has a dry seat. Keep him under control.

On leaving the marsh your dog will be cold and wet. Consider his needs before your own.

Pay special attention to cleaning your gun – saltwater will quickly corrode it; sand will also effect damage.

From time to time look through your gun barrels to make sure they are clear of mud or any other obstruction.

Do not shoot too early or at out-of-range birds: accurate judging of ranges will come with experience.

Send your dog to retrieve birds as they are shot, unless they are dead and easily recoverable later. 'Dogging' the tideline may recover lost birds.

Never leave litter such as cartridge cases or unsightly pit holes on the marsh.

1. This section was originally published by the British Association for Shooting and Conservation to whom grateful acknowledgement is made.

Do not try to be clever and wait until the last moment before leaving the marsh, when the tide is flooding. Channels will fill very quickly and in a very short time they can become a torrent, too deep to wade.

If you are uncertain about the identity of any bird – do not shoot it.

It is silly and wasteful to shoot any wildfowl that you or anyone else do not wish to eat or which cannot be picked up from the tideway.

If you are using a punt or boat make sure it is seaworthy and that you have paddles/oars, anchor, baler, life-jacket and emergency flares.

Golden plover (*top left*), Snipe (*top right*), Great Snipe (*lower left*)
and Jack Snipe (*bottom right*)

SURFACE-FEEDING DUCKS

MALLARD
Male: Green head, white neck-ring.
Female: Some orange on bill, whitish tail.

PINTAIL
Male: Needle tail, neck-stripe.
Female: Grey bill, slender pointed tail.

GADWALL
Male: Grey body, black rear.
Female: Yellowish bill, white speculum (in flight).

WIGEON
Male: Rufous head, creamy crown.
Female: Short blue-grey bill, light shoulders (not often visible when swimming).

SHOVELER
Male: Spoon-bill, dark chestnut sides.
Female: Spoon-like bill, blue shoulders (in flight).

MANDARIN
Male: Orange 'side-whiskers', orange 'sails'.
Female: White mark around eye, white chin.

TEAL
Male: Small; grey with dark head, horizontal white stripe above wing.
Female: Small size, green speculum.

GARGANEY
Male: White stripe on head, bluish shoulder-patch.
Female: From Teal by greyer wings, obscure speculum.

MARBLED DUCK
Mediterranean. Dappled plumage. Dark smudge through eye, white tail.

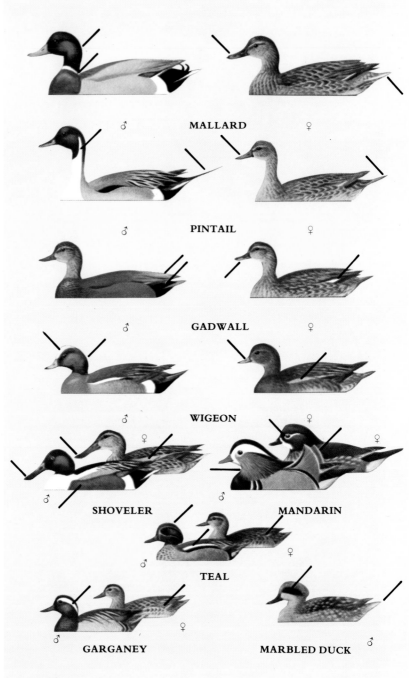

MALLARD ♂ ♀

PINTAIL ♂ ♀

GADWALL ♂ ♀

WIGEON ♂ ♀

SHOVELER ♂ ♀

MANDARIN ♂ ♀

TEAL ♂ ♀

GARGANEY ♂ ♀

MARBLED DUCK ♂

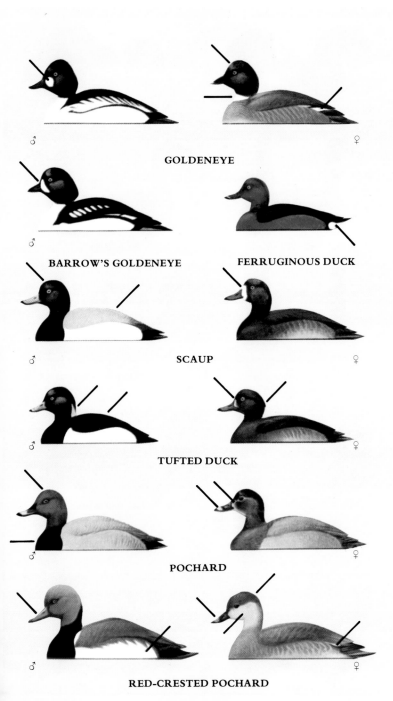

♂

GOLDENEYE

♀

♂

BARROW'S GOLDENEYE

FERRUGINOUS DUCK

♂

SCAUP

♀

♂

TUFTED DUCK

♀

♂

POCHARD

♀

♂

RED-CRESTED POCHARD

♀

DIVING DUCKS

GOLDENEYE
Male : Round white spot before eye.
Female : Grey body, brown head, white collar, white on wing visible when swimming.

BARROW'S GOLDENEYE
Iceland.
Male : White crescent on face; blacker above than Goldeneye.
Female : Very similar to Goldeneye.

FERRUGINOUS DUCK
Male : Deep mahogany; white under tail-coverts.
Female : Similar, but duller.

SCAUP
Male : Black foreparts, pale back, blue bill. 'Black at both ends, white in middle.'
Female : Sharply defined white patch at base of bill.

TUFTED DUCK
Male : Black foreparts, black back, drooping crest.
Female : From female Scaup by suggestion of crest. White at base of bill restricted or absent.

POCHARD
Male : Grey; black chest, rufous head.
Female : Buff mark around eye and base of bill, blue band on bill.

RED–CRESTED POCHARD
Male : From Pochard by red bill and white sides.
Female : White cheek, dark crown; from female Common Scoter by white wing-patch, red on bill.

GREY GEESE

Grey Geese with ORANGE Legs

WHITE-FRONTED GOOSE
Pink bill with white patch around base; black blotches on belly.

GREENLAND WHITE-FRONTED GOOSE
A subspecies; winters mostly in Ireland and western Scotland. Darker; bill yellow.

BEAN GOOSE
Bill yellow with black markings, but variable.

LESSER WHITE-FRONTED GOOSE
Smaller; stubby bill, *yellow ring* around eye. White more extensive on forehead. A distinct species.

Grey Geese with PINK legs

PINK-FOOTED GOOSE
Small; dark neck, bill black and pink.

GREYLAG GOOSE
Large and pale; bill has no black.

WESTERN GREYLAG
(The subspecies occurring in Britain.) Darker; orange-yellow bill.

EASTERN GREYLAG
Paler, with broad, light feather edges; pink bill.

Juv

Adult
WHITE-FRONTED

Greenland form

LESSER WHITE-FRONTED

BEAN

Adult — Juv

WHITE-FRONTED GOOSE

GREENLAND WHITE-FRONTED GOOSE

BEAN GOOSE

LESSER WHITE-FRONTED GOOSE

Eastern form

Western form

PINK-FOOTED GOOSE

GREYLAG GOOSE

PINK-FOOTED

Western — Eastern

GREYLAG

15
Ducks, Geese, Swans and Waders

Ducks, geese and swans belong to the family *Anatidae*; they are all waterfowl and have a worldwide distribution. The family comprises two sub-families, *Anatinae* – the ducks, and *Anserinae* – the swans and geese. Some of the species in each sub-family breed in Britain but much greater numbers visit our shores as migrants, either spending the winter in this country or passing through it on their journey between the northern breeding grounds and wintering areas further south and west. Characteristically, all are largely dependent for their survival on water, or land influenced by free water, such as fresh marshes, bogs, saltmarshes and the intertidal flats of mud and sand.

Other characteristic features of the sub-families include webbed toes to facilitate swimming, a well developed oil-gland above the parson's nose (or tail region) which produces the oil needed to maintain waterproofed plumage, and the annual simultaneous moult of the flight feathers which renders the bird flightless in mid-summer for about five weeks. During this period the males of those species, normally distinctively plumaged, moult into a drab 'eclipse' plumage which helps them to remain camouflaged from predators during this vulnerable period. Eclipse-plumage birds can be distinguished as the wings are the same pattern and colour throughout the year.

Swans and geese usually pair for life, although a lost mate is probably replaced. The ducks, however, normally pair in late winter but remain together only until the duck is incubating her eggs, when the drake will leave her. The young typically are covered with down and are active immediately after hatching; they do not return to the nest thereafter for they are brooded by the duck at night and in cold and wet conditions.

The Identification of Ducks

Habitat, action, colour, shape and voice all help distinguish one species from another. Particular attention should be paid to the following points: bill colour, leg colour and speculum (the colour of the wing patch). Some call notes which are rarely heard are confusing or too difficult to distinguish and therefore have not been included.[1]

Dabbling Ducks

These are typically birds of fresh, shallow marshes and rivers rather than of large lakes and bays. They feed, as their name suggests, by dabbling, that is, sifting through shallow water in search of vegetable and animal food and often upending in deeper water. Species such as mallard and teal will also feed on crop lands; cereal stubbles and potato fields are particularly favoured. The plumage of the ducks (females) generally is drab and hence gives camouflage but the drake (male) is boldly coloured. Only the female has a speculum, unless otherwise stated. They ride high in the water and launch themselves directly upwards when rising, whether from land or water.

Mallard (*Anas platyrhynchos*) A large duck. The drake has a glossy green neck and head, separated from greyish-brown mantle and rich chestnut breast-shield by a white ring; bill yellow, flanks and back light grey, black rump, white tail. The duck is predominantly brown with some orange on bill; whitish tail. Legs orange. Speculum large, violet-blue. Voice: a variety of 'quacks'.

Pintail (*Anas acuta*) A large, long-necked, graceful duck. Adult drake has grey flanks with cream band at rear and black rump, head and back of neck chocolate-brown, front of neck white for about two-thirds of its length and a thin white line running upwards to the level of, and behind, the ear; undersides white. Look for the central pair of tail feathers, elongated into the 'pin' or needle tail. The duck is predominantly brown with mottled brown belly, the bill is grey and the tail is slender and pointed. Speculum purplish-bronze. Voice: drake 'kruk'.

---

1. We have included illustrations of wildfowl with which we think the sportsman should be familiar. Some are protected, some partly protected. Because a species is included in this book it does not mean that it can necessarily be shot. Please refer to the text.

SHELDUCK

RUDDY
SHELDUCK

MALLARD

PINTAIL

WIGEON

SHOVELER

GARGANEY

TEAL

GADWALL

GOOSANDER

SMEW

RED-BREASTED MERGANSER

DABBLING DUCKS, SAWBILLS AND SHELDUCK

SHELDUCK
Black, white and rufous pattern, large white fore-wing patches.

RUDDY SHELDUCK
Pale cinnamon colour.

MALLARD
Dark head, two white borders on speculum, neck ring.

PINTAIL
Needle tail, one white border on speculum, neck stripe.

WIGEON
Large white shoulder-patches, grey back.

SHOVELER
Heavy spoon bill, large bluish shoulder-patches.

GADWALL
Largely white speculum.

GARGANEY
Small; large bluish shoulder-patches.

TEAL
Small, dark-winged; green speculum.

SMEW
White head and belly, white, fore-wing.

GOOSANDER
Merganser shape; white chest, large wing-patches.

RED-BREASTED MERGANSER
Merganser shape; dark chest, large wing-patches.

Wigeon (*Anas penelope*) A medium-sized duck, smaller than the mallard. The wigeon is unusual in that it is a grazing duck feeding on grasses, salt-marsh plants, etc. Adult drake (which is called a cock) has pale-yellow forehead and crown, rest of head and neck chestnut; back and flanks light grey, chest pinkish-brown; undersides white, black rump, striking white wing patch. The adult duck (hen) is predominantly brown with white belly, short blue-grey bill and feet and light shoulders. Speculum green, bordered white. Voice: the drake utters the familiar 'whee-oo', the duck produces a curious growling 'purr'.

Teal (*Anas crecca*) A small duck. The adult drake has head and neck rich chestnut on either side of a broad green marking from in front of eye to nape, back and flanks vermiculated grey, black-speckled pale breast, white underside, cream rump edged with black. The adult duck is sombre, sometimes greyish-brown, including belly, bill slate-coloured, legs greyish. Speculum green and black, bordered buff in front. Voice: drake utters a high pitched 'chirp', the duck a rather soft, high-pitched 'quack'.

Shoveler (*Anas clypeata*) A medium-sized duck, the adult drake having a glossy green head, neck and breast white, belly and flanks rich chestnut, dark back, white patch in front of rump, blue shoulders; bill black and longer than head, narrow at base, with characteristic 'spoon' bill; legs orange. Duck predominantly light brown, same spoonlike bill and blue shoulder patches, legs pale brownish-yellow. Speculum green edge, broad white in front and narrow white behind.

Gadwall (*Anas strepera*) Smaller than the mallard. Drake with chestnut and black shoulder patches, dark grey vermiculated chest and flanks, brownish back, pale head with dark crown and nape, black rump, pale undersides. Duck mottled brownish, belly whitish, bill dark grey with orange sides, narrower than mallard. Speculum white in both sexes. Legs pale brownish-yellow.

Garganey (*Anas querquedula*) Slightly larger than teal. In summer drake has broad crescent-shaped white eye-stripe on rich dark-brown head. Pale-blue shoulders which distinguishes the eclipse bird from teal, breast and rump brown and barred, flanks grey, belly white. Speculum green, edged white. Duck, grey-brownish, with white belly and lighter rump and chest. Speculum and shoulders less bright than drake; thin white eye-stripe well marked. The garganey is a summer visitor to Britain.
   A protected species.

Diving Ducks

These are closely related to dabbling ducks but frequent the larger, deeper lakes and rivers, coastal bays and inlets. They are adapted for swimming efficiently under water, often diving to considerable depths in search of food, their common diet being fish, shellfish, molluscs and aquatic plants. The wings are shorter and narrower than those of the dabbling ducks (their wing beats in flight are consequently more rapid) and their legs are set further back on the body and more to the sides. These ducks are less buoyant on the water and so give a lower silhouette. When launching into flight most of this group patter along the water before becoming airborne.

Goldeneye (*Bucephala clangula*) A medium-sized duck. Drake predominantly white with black back and rump, head glossy green with high forehead, circular white cheek-spot at base of bill, series of white bars on wing. Duck, head and neck warm earthbrown, eye-iris yellow, white collar, greyish breast extending to flanks, dark-grey back, bill slate, legs brownish-yellow, speculum white. Characteristic flight produces a loud rattle.

Scaup (*Aythya marila*) A medium-sized duck, larger than tufted. Adult drake, upper parts pale grey, vermiculated, black chest and rump, flanks and belly white, head and neck glossy black-green, eye-iris bright yellow. Adult duck, head and back dark brown, flanks and breast lighter brown, undersides pale, broad white facial band, eye-iris dark yellow, bill and legs grey, speculum white. Both sexes have white wing bar.
   A protected species

Tufted Duck (*Aythya fuligula*) A small duck. Adult drake, black with white flanks and belly and with long crest at back of head. Adult duck, back and head rich dark brown, crest on head shorter than in the drake, undersides and flanks pale, bill and legs greyish, speculum white. White wing bar on both sexes.

Pochard (*Aythya ferina*) A medium-sized duck. Drake is pale grey, black chest, white head and neck chestnut. Dark-brown duck has buff mark around eye and base of bill, grey undertail, reddish-chestnut head, legs bluish-grey, no wing bar. Bill of both sexes is slate-grey with black at base and tip.

DIVING DUCKS

TUFTED DUCK
Black back, broad white wing-stripe.

SCAUP
Grey back, broad white stripe on rear edge of wing.

FERRUGINOUS DUCK
Mahogany colour; wing-stripe.

POCHARD
Grey back, broad grey wing-stripe.

RED–CRESTED POCHARD
Broad white patch extends nearly length of wing.

GOLDENEYE
Large white wing-squares, short neck, black head with white spot. Wings whistle in flight.

LONG–TAILED DUCK
Dark unpatterned wings, white on body.

HARLEQUIN
Stocky, dark; small bill, white marks.

KING EIDER
White fore-parts, black rear-parts.

EIDER
White back, white fore-wings, black belly.

VELVET SCOTER
Black body, white wing-patches.

SURF SCOTER
Black body, white head-patches.

COMMON SCOTER
All-black plumage.

TUFTED DUCK

SCAUP

FERRUGINOUS DUCK

RED-CRESTED POCHARD

POCHARD

GOLDENEYE

LONG-TAILED DUCK

HARLEQUIN

KING EIDER ♂

EIDER

VELVET SCOTER

SURF SCOTER

COMMON SCOTER

Common Scoter (*Melanitta nigra*) The only all-black duck. A marine duck. Drake entirely glossy black, bill black with orange band and black knob at base. Duck, dark brown, belly paler, side of face and throat greyish-white, pale patch from below eye to halfway down neck, bill and legs slate-grey. Voice: drake, musical whistle, duck, a low growl.

A protected species

Velvet Scoter (*Melanitta fusca*) Similar to common scoter but both sexes have large white speculum; drake with white under eyes, legs and toes scarlet. Voice: rarely heard; whistle in courtship by both sexes.

A protected species

Long-Tailed Duck (*Clangula hyemalis*) A marine diving duck, flight strong, swinging from side to side, wings held downwards; often belly flops onto water. This species has unusual eclipse-plumage changes, with front half dark, except for large white face-patch. In normal plumage drake has white head and neck, chocolate cheek-patch, uniformly dark wings, chest and very long tail. Duck less contrasted and short-tailed. Bill and legs greyish, with orange on bill of drake.

A protected species

Common Eider (*Somateria mollissima*) A heavily built marine duck. Drake with black belly, flanks and rump, white breast and back, black crown and green on nape. Duck mottled dark brown. Bill, legs and feet greyish. Voice: drake 'coo-ru-hu', duck, a harsh 'korr'.

A protected species

Sawbills

These exhibit characteristics of diving ducks but, in addition, are adapted to fish eating and have narrow serrated bills.

Red-Breasted Merganser (*Mergus serrator*) A medium-sized duck. Drake, double-crested glossy green head, neck white with dark line down the back, breast brown, striated back, wings and back boldly marked in black and white, with conspicuous white patches in shoulder region. Underparts white, washed with rose-pink. Duck, rather as goosander, but upper parts browner. Both sexes bill red, speculum white.

Protected in England and Wales, subject to limited exceptions in Scotland

Goosander (*Mergus merganser*) A large sawbill. Drake, head with rounded crest, glossy green, rest of bird mainly white, with black back, lower neck and underparts pale salmon-pink. Duck, head brown, throat white, upper parts grey, underparts pale salmon-pink. Both sexes, bill red and speculum white.

Protected in England and Wales, subject to limited exceptions in Scotland

Smew (*Mergus albellus*) A small sawbill, little larger than teal. Drake, mainly white, grey flanks, black on back and wings, black from eye to base of bill, crest on front of head. Duck, crown and back of neck fox-red, white under chin, upper parts grey, underparts and speculum white, flanks grey, bill short, stout, grey-black.

A protected species

Shelduck

These are an intermediate between ducks and the true geese and exhibit some characteristics of both. For example, the male and female are similar in appearance. Shelduck have a mainly white body, dark blackish-green head, neck and shoulders, chestnut band around body in front of wings, chestnut patch under tail, red bill. Voice: drake, a whistle during courtship, duck, a laughing series of croaks.

A protected species

Perching Ducks

In this country these are represented only by the mandarin (*Aix galericulata*) and the carolina (*Aix sponsa*) both of which have been introduced.

Both are protected species

The Identification of Geese

Within the sub-family *Anserinae* the geese are commonly divided into the genus *Anser*, more commonly called 'grey' geese, and *Branta* or 'black' geese. The former comprise such species as the greylag, pink-footed and white-fronted geese and the latter comprise the Canada, barnacle and brent geese. Most species are winter visitors, although resident populations of greylag and Canada geese are now widespread.

There are no obvious plumage differences between the sexes as there are in ducks. The most certain points for identification of the geese are the colour of the bill, legs and the call notes. Young birds generally are like adults in their plumage, although duller. Within the wintering flocks the bond between young and adult birds is strong. Characteristically, such flocks fly in 'V' formations or straggly lines known as 'skeins'. Geese are vociferous. Once different call notes have been learned they can be identified at great distances.

The grey geese are mainly associated with marshes, pastures and arable land. The black geese, brent and barnacle, are mainly coastal birds although both species now feed inland as well.

Grey Geese

Greylag (*Anser anser*) The largest grey goose – up to 9½lbs(4.5kg) in weight. Plumage, overall light grey with pink legs, pale-grey fore-wings, large orange bill with white nail. Blue-grey shoulders are distinctive. Voice: similar to that of the farmyard goose, 'ank ank' or 'arne'.

Pink-Footed (*Anser brachyrhynchus*) A smaller, darker goose than the greylag, with pink legs and feet, dark head and neck, bill pink with black markings. Voice: a sharp 'wink wink' call in flight.

European White-Fronted (*Anser albifrons*) Legs orange-yellow, bill pink and shorter than the Greenland race. Adults have white feathers from base of bill to forehead, though not as far as the eye. The breast is heavily barred with black markings. Plumage, greyish-brown. Winters in England and the Welsh border.
  Protected in Scotland

Greenland White-Fronted (*Anser flavirostris*) Legs orange-yellow, bill yellow, longer than European form. Plumage much darker, can appear almost black. Winters in north and west Scotland, west Wales and Ireland. Voice: call notes of both races, 'kow, yow, yow'.
  Protected in Scotland

Lesser White-Fronted (*Anser erythropus*) A small goose, accidental visitor. Very short pink bill, legs orange, white 'front' extends to above eyes. Eyelids yellow.
  A protected species

SWANS AND GEESE

BEWICK'S SWAN
Adult: Base of bill yellow.
Immature: Dingy; bill dull flesh to base.

WHOOPER SWAN
Adult: Yellow on bill more extensive, forming point.
Immature: Larger than Bewick's, longer neck.

MUTE SWAN
Adult: Bill orange, with knob.
Immature: Bill flesh, black at base.

SNOW GOOSE
Adult: White, with black wing tips.
Immature: Dingier; bill dark.

BARNACLE GOOSE
Black chest and neck, white face.

CANADA GOOSE
Black neck, light chest, white cheek-patch.

BRENT GOOSE
Black chest and neck, small white neck-spot. Immature birds lack the neck-spot.
Dark-bellied form: Dark under-parts. In Britain, mainly East and South coasts.
Light-bellied form: Light under-parts. In Britain, mainly West, especially Ireland.

RED-BREASTED GOOSE
Chestnut breast, broad white flank-stripe, head pattern.

Juv Juv Juv
Adult Adult Adult
BEWICK'S   **WHOOPER**   **MUTE**

MUTE SWAN

WHOOPER SWAN
BEWICK'S SWAN

Adult

SNOW GOOSE

BARNACLE **GOOSE**

CANADA **GOOSE**

Light-bellied form

Dark-bellied form

BRENT GOOSE

RED-BREASTED GOOSE

Bean (*Anser fabalis*) Rare winter visitor. Legs orange. Bill orange with black markings. Plumage somewhat darker than greylag or pink-footed; size approximate to greylag.

A protected species

Black Geese

Canada (*Branta canadensis*) The largest British goose, black neck, light chest with white check patch, black tail, white rump, weight 10–15lbs(4.5–6.8kg). Voice: well named 'the honker', the notes a loud and ringing 'ah honk', with emphasis on the 'honk'.

Brent (*Branta bernicla*) Predominantly grey and black with a semi-collar of white marking on either side of the neck. Commonly found amongst coastal marine habitat although, in recent years, they have increasingly become partially an inland species by crossing the sea wall. Two forms frequent the British Isles, the dark-bellied and the light-bellied brent goose, the latter being more numerous in Ireland. Voice: low-pitched metallic, carrying a long way.

A protected species

Barnacle (*Branta leucopsis*) A very distinctive goose, predominantly black, silvery grey and white. Adults, head, neck and upper breast black except for face which is creamy white; bill, legs and feet black, white rump, black tail. Seldom fly in formation but in loose pack. Voice: yapping call, similar to small dogs.

A protected species (but they can be shot – under licence – in areas where they are causing serious crop damage).

Swans

Three species are found in Britain: the mute, which is resident, and the whooper and bewick's which are winter visitors. They frequent fresh and brackish water, floods, tidal estuaries and some coast.

Swans also fly in 'V' formation and the wing beats of the mute swan make a singing sound, whereas those of the whooper and bewick's swans are silent.

All swans are protected

The Identification of Waders

Particular attention should be paid to the colour of the legs, bill, speculum, size and shape. Some call notes also aid identification.

Most waders are wholly or partially migratory and large numbers both winter in Britain and pass through the country in autumn and spring. During the winter months they frequent the intertidal zones or major estuaries, often flighting to adjoining farmland during the day. In summer the same species feed in habitats ranging from saltmarshes to upland and moorland.

Waders

Golden Plover (*Pluvialis apricaria*) In winter upper parts gold and sepia, underparts white. Bill short. No wing bar. A bird of the shore and of arable land, especially ploughed fields. Voice: a clear piping 'thui'.

Snipe (*Gallinago gallinago*) Slim, medium-sized wader with a dark appearance. Back with strong buff stripes, paler underside. Long straight bill. More often found on fresh marshes than on the shore. Characteristically, has erratic flight. Voice: nasal 'scrape' call in flight. A Game Licence is required before shooting snipe.

Golden plover and snipe are the only two waders, apart from woodcock, which may be shot.

Common Protected Waders

Curlew (*Numenius arquata*) The largest wader, brown above with white rump, long down-curved beak. Legs slate-coloured. A bird of the mudflats, coastal pastures and moors, gull-like in flight. Voice: clear and loud 'curlee' and a long bubbling trill.

Redshank (*Tringa totanus*) A medium-size wader of the mudflats and saltmarshes. Light brown, orange-red legs, black-and-white barred tail. Bill red at base, straight and long. Legs and feet red, projected beyond tail in flight. In flight white rump and back are visible and white trailing edges of wings. Voice: very vociferous, when alarmed 'tu, hu, huhu'.

Jack Snipe (*Lymnocrytes minimus*) About half the size of the common snipe, with very dark appearance and contrasting stripes on back. Narrow wing bars and very little white in a rather pointed tail. Less erratic flight than common snipe.

Whimbrel (*Numenius phaeopus*) Half the size of the curlew. Brown above striated head pattern, centre of crown buffy-yellow, above eyes blackish and then buffy-yellow, rump white, tail barred brown. Long down-curved beak. Legs slate-coloured. A bird of mudflats and coastal pastures. Voice: high-pitched rapidly uttered whistle, repeated usually about seven times; also has bubbling song, similar to that of curlew.

Bar-Tailed Godwit (*Limosa lapponica*) Bill long and slightly upturned. Plumage greyish-brown striated. Rump white. No wing bar, tail white-barred, legs and feet grey and feet only just project beyond tail in flight. Frequents mudflats.

Black-Tailed Godwit (*Limosa limosa*) Black tail, broad white wing bar and legs which project beyond tail.

Woodcock (*Scolopax rusticola*) Refer to chapter twelve, 'Gamebirds and Woodcock'.

Other Protected Waders

Greenshank, oyster catcher,[1] avocet, green plover (or peewit), ringed plover, little ringed plover, Kentish plover, dotterel, dusky redshank, knot, turnstone, little turnstone, green sandpiper, purple sandpiper, wood sandpiper, common sandpiper, grey- and red-necked phalarope, dunlin, sanderling, curlew sandpiper, ruff (and reeve), stone curlew, black-winged stilt, great snipe.

For further note on wildfowl close seasons see page 28.

1. Oyster catchers may be shot in certain specified areas.

16

Wetland Habitats[1]

Waterfowl provide some of the most exciting shooting and live in what are called 'wetland' habitats. Waterfowl and wetland habitats are, of course, inseparably linked and their complex relationship can be described here only in the broadest outline. The main point is that if you have plenty of wetland habitat you are at least one step towards having plenty of waterfowl. If wetlands are being destroyed – 'in the national interest' it is sometimes claimed – it is a duty for shooters and conservationists to try to make good the loss and preserve the remainder, whenever possible.

Waterfowl can be defined as those birds which largely depend for their survival on water, or land influenced by free water, such as fresh marshes (where the soil is mostly mineral), bogs (where the soil is heavily organic or peaty), saltmarshes (where the land is regularly washed by the tide, but not so much that plants cannot grow) and the intertidal flats of mud and sand.

Waterfowl fall into six main groups: wildfowl (ducks, geese and swans); waders (such as redshank, curlew and snipe) that we have already described; gulls and terns; grebes and rails; some passerines (kingfisher, dipper and wagtails) and one raptor – the osprey.

The different wetland habitats can be described as salt water, fresh water or brackish (part salt water and part fresh water). Fresh water can be alkaline, neutral or acid, but alkaline waters are the most important to waterfowl for they are biologically more productive of food and cover. They are usually found in lowlands and fertile valleys. Acid waters on the other hand usually occur on high and peaty ground.

The sea is not officially defined as a wetland but several shallow coastal

1. This chapter was originally published by the British Association for Shooting and Conservation to whom grateful acknowledgement is made.

areas exist, off eastern Scotland and in the Baltic, which support immense numbers of sea-duck (scoters, long-tailed duck and eiders). Coastal waters may also be important feeding sites for waterfowl in times of hard weather when inland waters are frozen. Whilst most sea-duck are not legitimate quarry, nor are they very edible, their welfare is the concern of the hunter.

Given this background, this chapter outlines the main ways to protect and create wetland habitats. We shall consider saltmarshes, fresh and brackish marshes, natural lakes and ponds, artificial man-made waters such as reservoirs (for domestic and industrial water as well as farm irrigation), gravel and clay pits, and rivers.

Some waters are used for roosting only – geese by night and several species of duck by day, and here freedom from disturbance as well as shelter are the main factors.

On all these habitats some attributes are vital to waterfowl all the year round. These include plentiful supplies of food, adequate roosts and freedom from pollution and disturbance. Other values are important only during certain periods: such as islands and cover for spring breeding, the summer moult and shelter from severe weather in winter. If these considerations are understood and conditions improved, then the birds benefit. But the first priority is to preserve the places where they are still to be found.

Preservation of Wetlands

The preservation of wetland habitats is necessary because of four man-made menaces which damage or destroy a significant number of wetlands each year and also have widespread effects:

   i *reclamation* for what can be described as 'industry', that is, building ground, waste disposal, airports, oil refineries and power stations.
  ii *reclamation* for agriculture by the progressive construction of sea walls further and further seaward, the filling-in of farm ponds and the drainage of marshland.
 iii *pollution* arising from land-based industries which discharge effluents into the sea or river systems, and from oil washed in from the sea – often from spillage.
  iv *disturbance* due to excessive use of areas by people through bird-watching, fishing, recreational activities such as dog-walking and horse-riding, sailing, water-skiing, power-boating and other water sports and, of course, wildfowling.

Where land-use policy is concerned it is usually a question of priorities and farming is, of course, vitally important. But although making agriculture efficient is a national priority, the few areas identified as being of national or international importance should not be sacrificed.

Most farms suffer from shortage of water, particularly in eastern counties. Efficient marsh drainage, which results in management-cost economies, stops the marsh acting like a sponge and makes it necessary to construct expensive reservoirs. These can support wintering and breeding waterfowl even though land use has changed drastically nearby. Where drainage takes place the water table is progressively lowered to reduce the chances of flooding and to make the use of agricultural machinery possible; cereals, brassicas, potatoes and even flower bulbs may then be cultivated.

The farmer should welcome *reasonable*, but not excessive, numbers of wildfowl and should help preserve important habitats. Ducks, geese and even swans feeding on crop wastes after harvest can remove old and diseased potatoes, grain and weeds. Grazing on winter wheat and spring grass can encourage shoot production and even increase the yield per acre. Wildfowl droppings may be selectively sought by cattle and sheep to make good nutritional deficiencies. If geese become damaging, however – and this does happen – and a farmer decides to use scaring devices or to shoot, he should do so as soon as they move onto a vulnerable crop and not wait until they have established themselves there.

Our environment contains many pollutants, most of them designed to kill specific animals and plants, but often with lethal or sub-lethal effects over a wide spectrum of life. Other pollutant chemicals such as oil, detergents and degreasing fluid may be distributed by accident or negligence. Even the lead shot used by sportsmen could be called a pollutant.

Insecticides such as DDT, BHC, aldrin, dieldrin, endrin, heptachlor and other organochlorines and organophosphates, cause problems by taking many years to break down and disappear from the environment. They may, therefore, also become accumulated in a food-chain; that is, when a low level of poison in a prey species builds up to a lethal concentration in the predator which eats it. The viciousness of such insidious poisons is not in doubt. The sportsman has a vital role to play, keeping a watch for affected birds and helping in monitoring projects when requested.

Oil pollution is now a major threat, causing immense numbers of casualties amongst seabird populations each year. Apart from tanker collisions and sinkings the main threat comes from illegal tank washing at sea. This results in the discharge of an oily sludge which clogs the bird's feathers and digestive tract.

Disturbance to wildfowl is very difficult to assess but a number of general observations require to be made. Disturbance of a diffuse nature is not necessarily bad. But when disturbance makes important waterfowl feeding and roosting areas uninhabitable at the critical times, then restrictions will be necessary. Controlled shooting is not necessarily detrimental as birds, particularly those which are not being shot at, quickly become used to the sound of nearby gunfire. On the other hand, the irresponsible birdwatcher or photographer, who pays little for his privilege, can also unwittingly cause a lot of damage by creating disturbance.

Fishermen are realistic people, often good naturalists and sometimes also keen shots. They may have to pay large sums of money for their sport. There can, however, be some conflict between fishing and wildfowling interests. Game fishing which takes place mainly during the nesting season may cause disturbance to nesting duck and to young ducklings which need to be brooded in peace. The trampling of nesting cover can also be a problem. Game fishing during September, and particularly coarse fishing during the winter months, can cause disturbance of the day roosts and resting places, which may result in a serious fall-off in the numbers of waterfowl.

Advice on the management of schemes for meeting the complex requirements of ensuring the continuation of regulated wildfowling in valuable wetland habitats is available from the BASC: techniques have been developed as a result of years of co-operation with important nature-conservation interests on national and local nature reserves.

Creation of Wetlands

In this country the large coastal wetlands do not lend themselves to improvement in the same way as ponds, lakes or even snipe marshes. Practical habitat management on saltmarshes centres on controlling sheep-grazing to produce good swards, particularly of wigeon grass (*Puccinellia*). The control of cord grass (*Spartina*) can also be undertaken where it overruns mud and sand on which estuarine birds find food.

Operations on a large scale on inland marshes, involving the use of machinery to produce shallow flooded scrapes or impoundments, are specialist projects and must be carried out only after careful planning and consultation with technicians.

Small ponds and marshes can be created quite simply and at little cost. If fed and used as flight ponds they *must* be shot with great restraint. Otherwise more than a fair harvest of the surplus stock may be taken. Great care should be taken since flight ponds can draw ducks from a very wide area and a proportion may have been born as far away as Russia. If flighting ducks are fed artificially, this practice should be maintained after the end of the shooting season so that breeding birds, whether local or migratory, will be in good condition. It is important, however, that such artificial methods should not harm the natural value of the site. For example the dumping of excessive loads of food can attract rats and putrify the water. During the nesting season everything possible should be done to ensure breeding success.

Those who use flight ponds can replace at least a proportion of those ducks shot during the winter, by rearing some artificially. The stock must be from a hardy strain, released with care and fed correctly after release. Inland lakes and ponds can support hand-reared broods of wildfowl to supplement the wild populations on surrounding wetland areas.

The scope for improving fresh-water wildfowl habitat is considerable. The main requirements are:

i   A secluded home range where both ducks and geese spend most of their time in late winter and early spring before nesting, or before migrating to their breeding grounds.
ii   The nest site.
iii The brood-rearing area or duckling-survival habitat.
iv   The moulting and loafing spots.
v   The winter day-roost (or night-roost for geese) area with protection from disturbance.
vi   Flight-feeding areas which may be wetlands or agricultural crops.

The banks of all ponds and lakes should be gently sloped to about 16ins(0.4m) depth so as to make dabbling possible and to facilitate planting of cover and food species. Also included should be a gentle underwater slope (from about 5ft(1.5m) depth upwards) for emergent plants which also provide food and shelter, particularly for ducklings. There should be areas of open water about 8ft(2.5m) deep if diving ducks, grebes, etc. are being catered for and to ensure that the pond is not over-run by emergent plants and that the water stays fresh in summer. A steep bank may mean that ducklings will perish because they cannot reach dry ground for being brooded, or they may become separated from their mother duck.

Spits should be constructed to lengthen and break up shorelines to improve brood-rearing success; and, by shielding neighbouring birds, provide more territories for the drakes, thereby increasing the number of home ranges on the site.

Natural islands are a great asset. Artificial islands can be built to provide shelter and dabbling areas. They will be favoured nesting sites if there is protection from the elements and predators. Islands need to be about 16–22ft(15–20m) apart and can be as little as 1–2ft in diameter, although larger ones are usually more stable. They should be sited in sheltered areas so as to reduce erosion of their banks. Islands also help to dispose of surplus soil and reduce the cost of soil-moving when a pond is being constructed.

Floating raft islands for nesting are effective for several species of waterfowl, including ducks, geese, grebes and common terns.

Suitable loafing spots need to be free from tall vegetation so loafing birds have good all-round visibility, and there is nothing to conceal the approach of a predator. A duck likes to be able to swim ashore to a sheltered area where it can preen, sunbathe and sleep in security.

Planting

The objectives of planting are for the provision of foods, cover for nesting and moulting, shelter from the elements, enrichment of water and, finally, for landscaping and amenity.

In planting water margins the aim should be to reproduce a natural zonation of plants through the shoreline: terrestrial, marginal, floating aquatic and submerged species of plants; and a natural zoning of plants down the shore.

The plants should be represented by three different groups:

i Terrestrial trees, shrubs and herbs which grow on dry ground and provide shelter and cover, e.g., alder, willow, dogwood, brambles and nettles.

ii Emergent reeds and grasses at the waterside, e.g., burr-reed, sedge, reedgrass and club rush.

iii Completely aquatic, submerged and floating species, e.g., pond-weed and stonewort.

Trees and shrubs should be planted in the autumn. Broadly speaking they must be divided into those which require dry ground and those which will thrive in a high water table. Choice of species is naturally governed by soil type, climate and the degree of exposure of the site. Other species may be established by transplanting rootstocks during the summer growing season, preferably before flowering.

17

Deer

While deer stalking is a sister sport to game shooting and wildfowling, it stands rather separate; not only because of the larger size of the quarry but also because the weapon used is the rifle not the shotgun. No matter how competent anyone may be in the use of a shotgun he cannot, in any way, be considered qualified to shoot deer, either in woodland or on the hill, without further study and training.

From the point of view of safety alone the lethal range of a rifle so far exceeds that of a shotgun that shotgun-safety standards, no matter how stringent, in no way measure up to those required for the safe use of the rifle. The actual technique of stalking can best be learned by accompanying a professional or experienced stalker; but, sooner or later, the beginner will be out on his own, in a situation very different from pigeon shooting or taking a spaniel into rough cover to collect a brace of pheasants for the pot. Close study of the following pages should prevent the commission of the worst errors and allow even the early expeditions to be both enjoyable and successful.

The Development of Deer

In the United Kingdom there are, at present, six species of deer in the wild. They are red deer, fallow, roe, sika, muntjac and Chinese water deer. Each species will be described separately; but first, two points common to most of them will be covered.

Antler Growth With the exception of Chinese water deer, the males of all British species grow antlers from a part of the skull termed the *pedicles*.

These antlers are dropped or cast and regrown normally every twelve months (see Figure 1). Deer of the same species usually cast and regrow at approximately the same time each year. Muntjac are exceptional in that they may cast at any time of the year. During regrowth, which starts as soon as the antlers are cast, they are covered with a soft, furry skin known as *velvet*. When the antlers are fully developed this velvet shrivels, dries and is rubbed off on convenient bushes. This is called 'fraying' and, when it is completed, the animal is said to be *clean* or *in hard horn*.

In normal conditions, the antlers increase annually in size, in the number of points and in thickness, until the animal reaches its prime, when they start to deteriorate; at this stage a deer is said to be 'going back'. But the improvement of the antlers depends not only on age and sexual maturity but also upon environmental conditions.

Ageing It is fair to say that the size and shape of a deer's antlers give an indication of its age, but it is dangerous to go further than that. A bad winter and spring can result in many deer carrying 'heads' showing little or no improvement – possibly a deterioration – on the preceding ones. Very good conditions may induce abnormal improvement. The overall appearance and behaviour of the deer give a far better indication (see Figure 7). Deer development may be similar to humans:

Young	Slender, upright, alert but curious
Middle-aged	Plumper, nervous
Older	Thickset body, lower head carriage, shy and often a 'loner'
Very old	Loss of weight, stiff in the joints, low head carriage

These are guidelines. Only experience can teach.

No description of tracks, droppings and many other important field signs can be attempted in the limited space available. Indeed, as already said, there can be no substitute for an apprenticeship with an experienced stalker.

Weights given are 'clean', that is, after removal of entrails and stomach contents.

Red Deer (*Cervus elaphus*)

Weight (see photograph on page 136 and Figure 1) The average weight of a woodland stag is around 350lbs(160kg) and a hind about 245lbs(110kg). Hill deer vary greatly from one area to another, but stags average about 190lbs(86kg) and hinds at 80–90lbs(36–41kg).

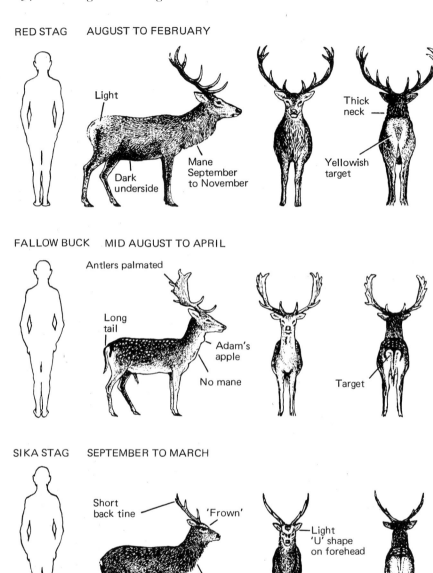

RED STAG   AUGUST TO FEBRUARY

Light

Dark underside

Mane September to November

Thick neck

Yellowish target

FALLOW BUCK   MID AUGUST TO APRIL

Antlers palmated

Long tail

Adam's apple

No mane

Target

SIKA STAG   SEPTEMBER TO MARCH

Short back tine

'Frown'

Short mane in autumn

Light 'U' shape on forehead

Gland

Figure 1 *Identification of red, fallow and sika deer (measured against a six-foot-tall man)*

STAG IN MARCH   HIND   CALF   HIND

Pedicles only

Short mane

Slender neck

Short brown tail

Long head

White spots

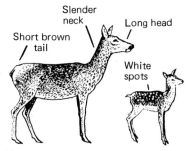

Light target

BUCK END OF APRIL   DOE   FAWN   DOE

Pedicles only

In both sexes many colour varieties occur, including all white and all black

White tail, black on top; long

STAG IN APRIL   HIND   CALF   HIND

Pedicles only

Ears more rounded than Fallow's

In both sexes body more thick set than Fallow's

Tail slightly shorter than Fallow's

Gland

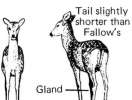

Red deer stag and hind at the rut

Pelage (coat) There are wide colour variations at all seasons, ranging from almost grey to nearly buff. The undersides and insides of the thighs are a creamy yellow, but in life this is rarely visible. There is a creamy *caudal* disc and a clearly visible tail about 6ins(150mm) long. A dark *dorsal* stripe is sometimes found. Stags grow a noticeable mane during the rut, which is retained throughout the year by older animals. The winter coat is thick, rough and often dirty looking. Calves are dark brown with white spots, which disappear at about six weeks.

Antlers The massive heads commonly seen in parks and on the Continent are rare in the wild in Britain. Hill stags frequently never produce more than a terminal fork above the two or three lower points; elegance rather than complexity is to be looked for by the trophy hunter or the stalker shooting selectively with the object of improving the standard of heads.

Habitat The red deer are naturally animals of woodland and the rough country adjoining. Where the forest has been removed, as in the Highlands of Scotland, they have adapted to the open hills. In hot weather they frequent higher ground where it is cooler and where insect attack is less. In winter they normally seek more sheltered areas, sometimes travelling long distances.

Voice Generally silent, compared with some other species. Both sexes, the hinds especially, bark to warn of danger. Hinds and calves communicate by bleating. During the rut the stags give a wide variety of 'roars', which generally resemble the bellow of a bull and frequently end with a series of grunts. Woodland stags sometimes give single resonant groans at long intervals.

Gait[1] (see Figure 2) When alarmed red deer usually move at a trot. This is smooth and rhythmic, with the head carried high and steady, and is very characteristic of the species. In dense cover the stags often throw back their heads until the antlers lie along both sides of the body. Depending on the circumstances and the degree of alarm the trot can break into a canter or gallop or be reduced to a walk. Red deer are excellent jumpers.

Food and Feeding Very catholic feeders, almost any palatable grass, shrub or tree is grazed or browsed. Acorns, beechmast, sweet chestnuts,

---

1. Gait is only described where it is especially distinctive.

Red stag

Fallow buck

Roe buck

Muntjac buck

Figure 2 *Gait of red stag, fallow buck, roe buck and muntjac buck*

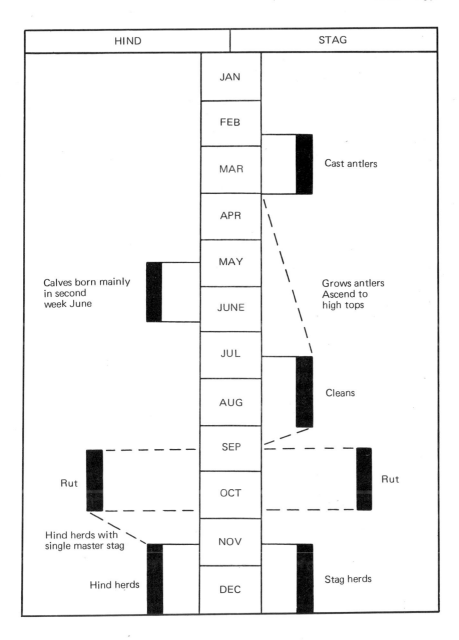

Figure 3 *The seasonal behaviour of red deer*
Often in summer and regularly in winter mixed herds of stags and hinds with calves and young deer can be seen together in the Highlands. Only in late spring and early summer are stags and hinds separated

hawthorn and rowan berries are taken in the autumn. Ivy and yew are eaten in winter. The species is very prone to marauding onto farm land, especially in search of root crops and spring corn. Hill deer eat various shrubs, heather and coarse grasses and, if near the sea, will visit the shore after seaweed. They are rough and noisy browsers, tearing down twigs and using their antlers to break off branches to a height of over six feet. Serious damage is done to pole-stage trees by bark-stripping.

Habits and Herd Activities Gregarious, but the herd structure changes throughout the year and varies from woodlands to the open hill. Sometimes stags and hinds herd together but usually mature stags form separate groups. During the rut senior stags attempt to monopolize as many hinds as possible. Fights, varying from a single threatening charge to lengthy struggles, are common. As the rut proceeds younger and smaller stags tend to take over the harems of the larger animals as the latter become run. A stag is in his prime between 10 and 13 years of age.

Wallowing in peaty or muddy pools is a much favoured occupation of both sexes. Feeding usually takes place early in the morning or at night, while the day is spent lying up in dense cover or reasonably fly-free areas. When possible these 'lying-up' areas are chosen to provide a wide field of view. In the Highlands it is common for deer to move down to the valley bottom for the better feed in the evenings, returning to higher grounds in the morning.

Seasonal/Social Behaviour (see Figure 3) Geography and habitat induce wide variations.

Fallow Deer (*Dama dama*)

An introduced species, present in British woodlands at least since Norman times and currently the most widely distributed feral deer in Britain.

Weight The buck up to 200lbs(90kg); the doe between 66lbs(30kg) and 110lbs(50kg).

Pelage Wide colour variations, with four main types (see photographs opposite and overleaf and Figure 1):
Common Summer coat is chestnut, with prominent white spots. Caudal disc white, clearly defined by circumferential black line which extends

Fallow doe with two fawns (twins are unusual)

down the long (9ins/230mm) tail. Winter pelage is grey-brown with barely visible spots. Light underside.

Melanistic Varies from black to very dark chocolate at all seasons. Some lightening of underside. Caudal disc dark.

Menil Very light-brown coat with numerous spots. Only British deer to remain heavily spotted in winter. Caudal disc has incomplete brown outline.

White Pale cream to pure white. Not albino, so appendages normal.

The first two varieties are commonest in the wild. The larynx (Adam's apple) and the penis sheath of hair (*tassel*) are prominent in the buck.

Antlers The characteristic heavy palms, absent in the young bucks most commonly sighted, may remain deficient or heavily fissured even in mature wild heads.

Habitat Extremely adaptable. Prefers mixed lowland woods with scope for internal browse and external grazing, but large woods inessential.

Fallow buck

Voice Both sexes emit a crisp bark when alarmed. Does and fawns bleat. The rutting buck 'groans'. This oft-repeated, resonant nasal snort or belch carries well and is unmistakable.

Gait (see Figure 2) As well as the usual walk, trot and bounding gallop, fallow under tension or excitement indulge in a very characteristic 'pronking' gait – a high, bouncing canter with all four limbs held rigid.

Food and Feeding Basically grazers although they will also browse. Diet depends upon the season and is very catholic. Grasses and grain crops are preferred, but fresh shoots of many shrubs, beechmast and acorns are all eaten in season.

Habits and Herd Activities (see Figure 4) Very gregarious. Mixed herds common in winter but sexes tend to separate before the single fawn is dropped in late spring. Females reproduce at about their second birthday. In the rut the mature bucks mark out their stands: small trees and bushes

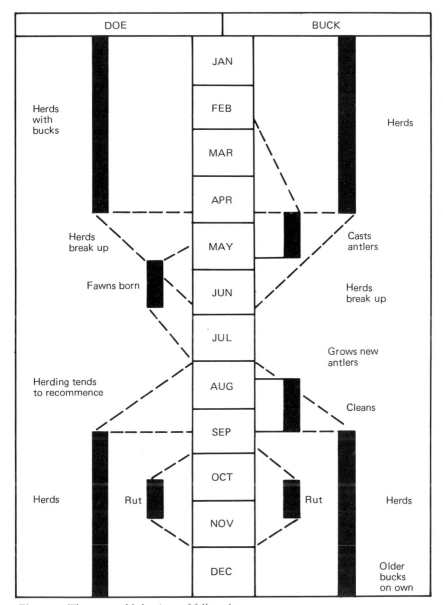

Figure 4 *The seasonal behaviour of fallow deer*

are thrashed with the antlers and deeply scraped hollows made in the woodland floor with the hooves. Here the bucks urinate and also set scent upon the herbage from the glands on the hocks and around the face. These pungent odours probably deter inferior bucks and attract the does who are commonly mated by the buck of their own choice. The master buck spends much time patrolling the perimeter of his area and chasing off juniors. He 'groans' almost continually and it is at this time that the stalker has his best chance to shoot a selected mature buck, preferably before his exertions cause him to lose condition.

Fallow are remarkably disease-free and tolerant of overcrowding. A buck is in his prime between eight and eleven years old. Few animals reach their late 'teens' as malnutrition sets in with the inevitable flattening of the molar and pre-molar teeth.

Seasonal/Social Behaviour (see Figure 4) Much depends upon the habitat in which the deer are living and particularly upon the amount of disturbance and persecution.

Sika (*Cervus nippon*)

Weight (see photograph below and Figure 1) Stags weigh about 130lbs(59kg) and hinds about 60–80lbs(27–36kg).

Pelage The summer coat is warm buff-brown (stags darker) with yellowish-white spots. Some variations in the degree of spotting, often forming a line high on the back. Light V-shape on forehead gives 'frown'

Japanese sika deer during rut

expression. Black dorsal stripe extends down the tail. In winter the coat turns to dark brown. Stags appear almost black. Spots much less evident. Caudal disc white bordered with black, flares into a large heart-shape when alarmed. Short tail white with dark stripe. Light patches on the outside of the lower part of the hind legs. Stags develop manes before the rut. Calves have browner coats than adults, fewer spots and much reduced rump patch.

Antlers The eight-point head is rarely exceeded in the wild though nine and ten pointers have been shot. Elaboration beyond the simple terminal fork raises suspicion of hybridization with red deer.

Habitat Sika prefer acid soils. By day lives mainly in dense thickets of many types, but also is found in marshy alder or reed beds. To avoid summer flies may take refuge in tall farm crops or visit open moors or heathlands.

Voice Alarm call of both sexes is a short screaming whistle ending with a grunt, often repeated several times with a short pause between each call. Hinds also bleat and bark. The rutting call of the stag is unmistakable. It consists of a loud whistle, rising to a high note and then declining down the scale to a concluding grunt. Usually repeated three times in rapid succession followed by silence for at least fifteen minutes. Other sounds produced by stags include a deep devilish chuckle and a peevish squeal.

Gait When suspicious sika, like other deer, tend to face the source of trouble, stamping a forefoot, peering and even advancing hesitantly. When moderately alarmed they bounce away, jumping with all four feet together. If seriously alarmed, however, they move off at a heavy bounding gallop.

Food and Feeding Predominantly grazers but also unselective browsers. Conifer needles are eaten as well as leaves of broad-leaf species. Hazel shoots are specially favoured. This species can damage forest trees, and raids farm crops. In coastal areas sea couch-grass is much sought.

Habits and Herd Activities Although sika are gregarious, herds are generally small. Stags and hinds mix during winter, but normally sexes live apart in small groups. Stags are very secretive. During the rut stags fight savagely for their hinds. Territories are marked by thrashing heather and bushes on the boundaries. Bole-scoring, pit-digging and wallowing are other notable rutting activities. Feeding is mostly at night with some crepuscular activity.

Seasonal/Social Behaviour (see Figure 5)

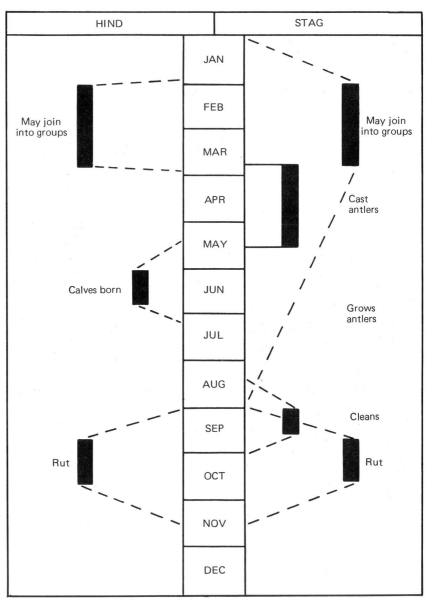

Figure 5 *The seasonal behaviour of sika deer*

Roe Deer (*Capreolus capreolus*)

Weight A good roe buck weighs 50–60lbs(22–27kg) and stands about
2ft1in–2ft5ins(635–736mm) at the shoulder. An average roe buck would
more likely weigh 40–45lbs(18–19kg). The doe weighs 6–12lbs($2\frac{1}{2}$–$5\frac{1}{2}$kg)
less and is shorter on the leg in proportion.

Pelage The summer coat is short and glossy; sandy to deep foxy red in
colour, shading to light buff on the underparts. During September and
October the darker winter coat develops: longer than the summer coat,
blackish-grey to warm brown in colour, often with one or two white
crescent patches on the throat. Caudal disc erectile: lemon-yellow to
brownish in summer and turning white in winter when the powder-puff
effect is startling. At this season the female shows a downward projecting
tuft of hair below the disc. There is no true external tail. The winter coat
falls in handfuls from mid–April. Yearlings are usually completely red by

Young roe buck and doe leaving cover

Roe deer are seasonal

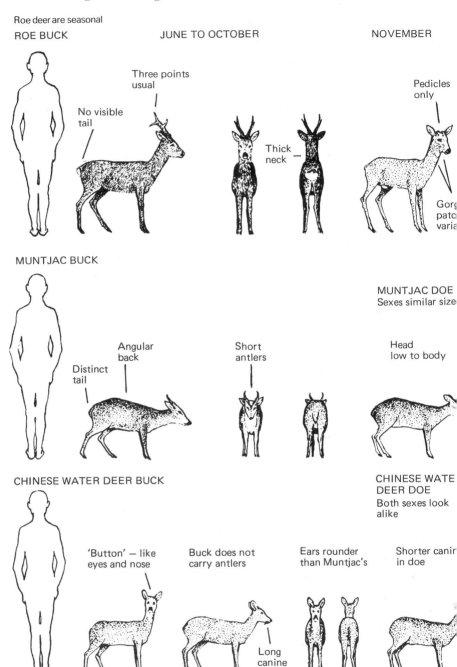

ROE BUCK   JUNE TO OCTOBER   NOVEMBER

Three points usual

No visible tail

Thick neck

Pedicles only

Gor
pat
vari

MUNTJAC BUCK

MUNTJAC DOE
Sexes similar size

Angular back

Distinct tail

Short antlers

Head low to body

CHINESE WATER DEER BUCK

CHINESE WATE
DEER DOE
Both sexes look alike

'Button' – like eyes and nose

Buck does not carry antlers

Ears rounder than Muntjac's

Shorter canin in doe

Long canine

Figure 6 *Identification of roe, muntjac and Chinese water deer*

ROE DOE IN JUNE
Sexes similar size

KID

DOE IN DECEMBER

Distinct white
tuft

Spotted

Slender
neck

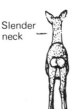

Short tail,
white underneath

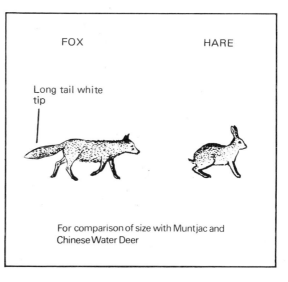

FOX

HARE

Long tail white
tip

For comparison of size with Muntjac and
Chinese Water Deer

mid-May; older animals may not be in full summer coat until the end of the month. The kids are born with a brownish or bluish coat with darker areas liberally splashed with white. These markings have virtually disappeared by the end of August.

Antlers Typical antlers have a total of six points: maximum length is about 12ins(304mm), although the majority are very much shorter, say 8–9ins(203–228mm). The nose is dark and moist with two white spots on the upper lip, the eye large and liquid. The prominent mobile ears are about $5\frac{1}{2}$ins(140mm) in length.

Habitat Prefers bushy cover, but is extremely adaptable. Roe can successfully live in suburban thickets, small woods, large conifer blocks and even open heather moorland.

Figure 7 *Ageing in roe buck*

Left: Young Roe buck.
Slender neck. Alert.
Juvenile behaviour.

Left lower: Middle age.
Plumper. Nervous.
Throws up head frequently.

Below: Old age. Thick-set body.
Firm rump.
When moving smells ground.
More shy.

Voice Bucks bark in challenge, and both sexes in alarm. Young roe scream when frightened or hurt, and there is a good deal of nearly inaudible murmuring, mainly between doe and fawn. In the rut, bucks bark and grunt.

Food and Feeding Roe are basically browsing animals, bramble and coppice growth being preferred foods. They will also feed on grass, corn and root crops and are capable of adapting themselves to a wide range of habitats.

Habits and Herd Activities (see Figure 8) The social unit consists of buck, doe and the doe's young of the year. The association is loose. As food and cover become more generally available in spring, mature bucks spend an increasing amount of time in their chosen territories. A buck often occupies the same territory for a number of years. Within this area he selects as fraying stocks small trees commensurate with his size and weight. The buck also paws the ground below the fraying stock, producing a triangular scrape, often marked with the imprint of his forefoot. Scraping as a method of territory marking begins before antler growth is complete. Scrapes can be found away from fraying stocks; usually where the roe have bedded. Bucks have scent glands in the skin of the forehead and face; they deposit these secretions on fraying stocks and also on low branches. The movement is comparatively gentle and can be readily distinguished from normal fraying. As spring progresses there is considerable competition for the most desirable territories.

Incursions into an occupied territory induce barking and fraying by the occupant. Usually the weaker animal retires, but savage fighting may occur between evenly matched bucks. Unsuccessful animals, chivvied constantly by the settled bucks, remain footloose throughout the summer. The majority of these bucks are juveniles, one or two years old.

The area which a doe favours may coincide with the territory of one buck or it may extend into the territory of a second. The kids of the previous year are chased away by their mother, usually in May. Both sexes are less aggressive in autumn and winter. If food becomes restricted to certain places, numbers of roe may be seen together but the loose family tie will still be apparent.

Roe are restless animals and where they are undisturbed their preference is to feed, rest and move about in short spells throughout the day and, when there is sufficient moonlight, at night. Human predation, however, has compelled them to adjust their timetable to peaks of activity at dawn and dusk.

Seasonal/Social Behaviour When the doe comes into season, usually in late July, she makes a high-pitched, squeaking noise. Any buck in the vicinity

Figure 8 *The seasonal behaviour of roe deer*

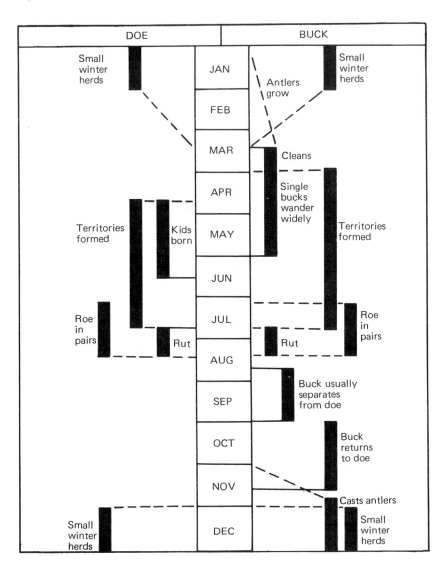

is immediately attracted. Bucks at this time are restless, sometimes even leaving their territories, and can be seen questing, nose to ground, fraying and barking without visible cause. As the doe becomes attractive, a prolonged courtship sometimes ensues, involving long, hectic chases.

Circular tracks called 'rings' are sometimes made by roe in this way. At the climax the doe will stand for the buck and he mounts her, often many times in the course of ten or fifteen minutes. Afterwards chasing may be resumed followed by further mating. The buck becomes exhausted but will not leave the doe as she will be quite willing to accept another male.

Pre-mating play is at a maximum in warm, sunny or thundery weather. The peak of the rut is usually around 4 August. Roe display the phenomenon of delayed implantation; this means that the embryo does not start developing until December following the rut. A period of renewed erotic behaviour around the end of September is known as the 'false rut', but only a small proportion of the roe population is involved. The young are usually born in May. In areas of high feeding most does produce twins, and triplets are sometimes reared, but natural wastage during the first year of life can be high: a 50 per cent loss is not unusual.

Muntjac (*Muntiacus reevesii*)

Weight (see photographs overleaf and Figure 6) The muntjac is a small, porcine deer. The buck weighs 25–30lbs(12–13kg); the doe is a little lighter (about 23lbs).

Pelage In summer the coat is a sleek glossy bay; in winter a duller brown. Chin and throat paler. Proportionately large tail, ginger above and white underneath; erected when the animal is alarmed. Fawns dark brown with light spots and chestnut stripe down back. Spots disappear after about eight weeks.

Antlers A short 2ins(50mm) incurved spike on a long pedicle.

Habitat Muntjac inhabit dense cover at most times; woods with heavy undergrowth such as brambles are preferred, but they will live temporarily in standing crops. They co-exist happily with humans in suitable habitat.

Voice Muntjac are noisy: both sexes give a loud single bark repeated at intervals of four–five seconds for long periods, even up to an hour; hence

Muntjac buck   *Muntjac doe*

their alternative name, 'Barking Deer'. They do this when disturbed, separated, excited or when does are in season. Does and fawns squeak if disturbed; a separated fawn utters a pathetic bleat. Muntjac also grunt and produce clicking sounds. They make a piercing and distressing cry when in extreme difficulty.

Gait (see Figure 2). At most times the head is carried low. Three gaits are common: a pottering walk while feeding desultorily; a swinging purposeful trot; and, when disturbed, a scampering run. Muntjac penetrate dense cover with ease and, for their size, jump extremely well, a 5-feet obstacle presenting no problem when thoroughly alarmed.

Food and Feeding Muntjac are mainly browsers with a very varied diet, exploiting any natural food in season, such as acorns and chestnuts. Little damage is done to farm crops but market gardeners and nurserymen suffer from their attacks. Only trivial forestry damage is done.

Habits and Herd Activities Muntjac live in family groups, consisting of the buck, doe, a juvenile and a fawn. The juvenile is expelled before a new fawn is dropped. Mutual grooming is frequent. Both sexes are potentially aggressive when fawns are small: cases are recorded of dogs being attacked on the lead. The long canine teeth, up to $1\frac{1}{2}$ins(38mm) are used for fighting and defence.

Seasonal/Social Behaviour Muntjac breed regularly and continuously, the does coming into season about twenty-four hours after fawning and gestating for about 210 days. Fawning and rutting consequently occur at any time of the year.

Chinese Water Deer (*Hydropotes inermis*)

Weight Average weight for both sexes is 25lbs(12kg). Bucks carry tusks up to 3ins(76mm) long; does $\frac{1}{2}$in(12.5mm) long (see photograph on page 157 and Figure 6).

Pelage Uniform sandy-chestnut colour. Quite dense coat. Winter coat very thick. Fawns are spotted until about three–four months of age. Sexes difficult to differentiate.

Antlers None.

Habitat Thin woodlands, fields with hedgerows, and especially marshlands.

Voice Normally very quiet. During July and August bucks walk about singly emitting a high-pitched scream – possible territorial behaviour. Under stress they also give a high-pitched scream and utter a bird-like chatter when fighting.

Gait Walks with a steady gait. On disturbance, runs off in huge leaps, kicking the hind legs higher than the back. Can jump 6 feet when alarmed.

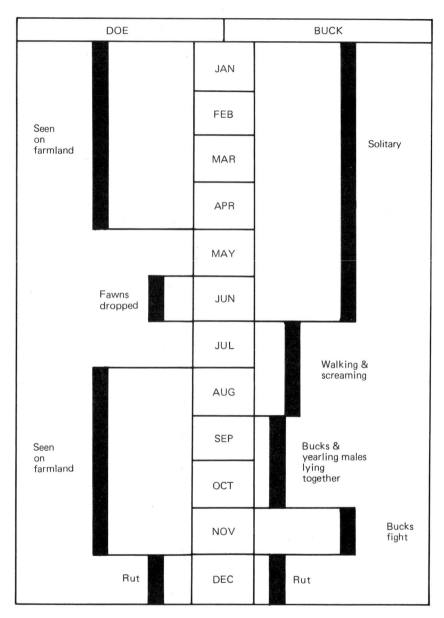

Figure 9 *Seasonal behaviour of Chinese water deer*

Food and Feeding Mainly grazers, favouring long grass, corn fields and sedges. As their stomachs are very small (only about six times as big as a rabbit's), they do little damage to crops.

Chinese water deer buck

Habits and Herd Activities The rut occurs during December with fierce fighting in November, the bucks slashing at each others' throats with their tusks. Does fawn from late May to early June after a gestation of twenty to twenty-two weeks. Multiple births of two or three are common. If in danger, bucks invariably run off; occasionally does will lower themselves on the forequarter and lie down. They do not defend themselves against humans or dogs.

Seasonal/Social Behaviour (see Figure 9)

18

Principles of Deer Management

The management of a deer population will vary, depending on the species of deer and the type of terrain. For example, the management of a red deer herd in a large Scottish deer forest under one owner differs widely from that of a lowland red or fallow herd ranging over numerous properties; both will differ from control of a small roe population living in one isolated wood. Any person embarking on deer management for the first time (no matter how small an area or population) should seek professional advice and should read the various authoritative publications on the subject. Only basic principles are given here.

Close Seasons All deer-management plans must, of course, conform to the statutory close seasons which are given opposite. These times are the periods laid down by law during which the animals may *not* be killed.

Population control

Population control should ensure that:
  i The health and quality of the deer are maintained and improved.
 ii The numbers of deer in any area are such that they have adequate natural food supplies throughout the year.
iii Serious economic damage by deer does not occur to agricultural and forest crops; that undue nuisance is not caused to garden owners; and that numbers do not present a traffic hazard.
 iv Culling of surplus deer is carried out humanely and efficiently within the terms of the Deer Acts; see chapter nineteen, 'Deer and the Law'.

Close Seasons for Deer

		JUN	JUL	AUG	SEPT	OCT	NOV	DEC	JAN	FEB	MAR	APR	MAY
MALES	Red					21							
	Fallow & Sika												
	Roe					21							
FEMALES	Red					20			16				
	Fallow & Sika					20			16				
	Roe					20							

Close season in:
England & Wales ▬▬▬ Scotland ••••••••••

The British Deer Society strongly recommends that both sexes of muntjac and of Chinese water deer should be granted a close season from 1 March to 31 October, for which there is, at present, no statutory close season.

Outline Management

In making a management plan the following should be considered in the order shown:

  i Range and ownership
 ii Holding capacity and damage potential
iii Census
 iv Sex balance
  v Making a cull plan
 vi Selection of culls

Range Deer do not neatly conform to property boundaries. As a first step it is essential to determine the range of any population and to involve as many individual property owners as possible in agreeing the management plan. Unless this is done, further steps will be pointless. With roe, which are territorial over small areas, consultation may involve only farmers immediately adjacent to the roe deer's home wood. On large Scottish deer forests consultation between two or three property owners may be sufficient. Lowland red, fallow and sika herds may cover a range of 100sq.miles(160sq.km), involving many separate blocks of woodland and numerous agricultural properties. Movement between different properties caused by availability of food, rutting habits, or by more than usual disturbance, may take place throughout the year. Management plans under these circumstances can present grave difficulties, best met by the formation of local Deer Control Societies. The initiative for the formation of such societies must come from the landowners themselves.

Holding Capacity and Damage Potential Having delimited the range, the manager must consider how many deer the ground can hold. Local knowledge is essential in determining such factors as:

i   How much food is available in woodland or on the hill, and how much is obtained from adjacent agricultural land?

ii What forest crops are at risk, that is, young plantations vulnerable to browsing or fraying, older stands of trees open to bark-stripping or areas of natural regeneration?

iii What amount of damage will the individual landowner allow?

The maximum holding capacity is the number of deer a given area will support in early spring when the natural food supply is at its lowest level and agricultural and forest crops at highest risk. Capacity will vary widely; as a very general guide the following figures may prove useful:

i   Red (hill) with no sheep competition or artificial feeding   1 deer to 50 acres of hill pasture

ii Red (lowland) with agricultural and forestry interests involved   1 deer to 200 acres of woodland

iii Fallow/sika with agricultural and forestry interests involved   1 deer to 150 acres of woodland

iv Roe with forestry interests involved   1 deer to 30 acres of woodland

These figures may require wide adjustment for particular situations. It is always better to understock. Overstocking induces disease problems; unacceptable damage; trophy deterioration; dispersal of the best animals (particularly males) and a peripheral overkill by poaching or semi-legal shooting out of season. Carrying capacities may be increased by improvement of the food supply, e.g., use of fertilizers, creation of deer lawns or by artificial winter feeding.

Census Having calculated the holding capacity, it is necessary to find out the numbers of deer on the ground. For roe in small areas, this can be done over a period of weeks by an individual observer. For red, fallow and sika, liable to move throughout their range, the census is best done over two or three consecutive days using sufficient observers to cover the whole range. With lowland animals an accurate assessment needs the co-operation of all landowners within the area. The use of helicopters or light aircraft with skilled observers would be ideal. The census should be taken by mid-April for lowland deer and late April to mid-May for hill deer. By then the bulk of the seasonal deaths from disease and malnutrition will have occurred; roe bucks will have established their territories and red/fallow/sika will have split into separate sex herds. Census figures should indicate totals of males and females, with an additional record of mature females of breeding age. Only experience can suggest what percentage must be added to account for deer not seen. It may vary from as low as 5 per cent for hill red deer to as high as 100 per cent for roe in thicket-stage woodlands. Especially with woodland deer the tendency is always to underestimate.

Sex Balance Before formulating the cull plan the manager must decide the sex balance. Ideally the ratio should be 1:1, male:female. In practice the proportion of females can be allowed to rise. The following figures may be useful:

i Red/sika   1 stag:1.5 hinds (excluding young of less than ten months)

ii Fallow/roe   1 buck:2 does

Cull Plan Having marshalled the facts the manager starts on the cull plan. With roe this involves making a separate one for each block of woodland. For the larger species, ranging over a number of properties, the plan should involve all the landowners. The aim is to leave a balanced population within the carrying capacity of the range. In making the plan the following factors must be considered:

i Carrying capacity	Population level to be achieved at completion of cull	
ii Census	Stock at present	
iii Annual increase	This must be added to the census total. It depends on the breeding success of the species involved and the habitat. As a very general guide, populations will increase (allowing for natural deaths) annually by:	
	Red (hill)	10–20 per cent depending on area and severity of winters
	Red (lowland)	30–33 per cent
	Sika	30–33 per cent
	Fallow	30–33 per cent
	Roe (southern)	40 per cent (approximately)
	Roe (northern)	20–25 per cent
iv Unnatural deaths	An estimate must be made of deer likely to be poached, shot on areas outside the manager's control, road casualties. This total must be deducted from the total potential stock (ii & iii).	

Having considered these factors, the manager can arrive at a total cull figure, that is ii+iii−iv=i. Before making a final decision he should, however, look ahead and consider whether any changes in either forestry or agriculture in the next three or four years are likely to affect the carrying capacity adversely. If so, he should plan to increase this cull now; to wait until the changes occur invites disaster. Having fixed overall cull figures a split must now be made between sexes. If an overall decrease of population is required a heavy female cull involving sexual imbalance is unavoidable temporarily. Finally, a cull plan should never be regarded as sacrosanct, it should always be under review.

Selection of Culls Weak, diseased or crippled animals of all age classes are obvious first choices for culling. These only fill a small part of any plan; the difficulties arise with the rest of the quota. Authorities agree that the bulk should be culled from animals below breeding age (nine months to two years) and from animals past their prime – the majority being taken from the more numerous first class. These two groups, combined with weaklings from the middle age group, provide the bulk of natural casualties. Neat pyramids can be drawn up showing the exact number of each age group to be culled. This is impossible in practice, except when dealing with very small populations under constant observation. Even experts cannot accurately age live, mature male deer to nearer than a bracket of two–three years. With females the problem is even more difficult; most professionals would agree that an animal can only be graded as young, middle-aged or old. A suggested cull break-down for both sexes could be:

i	Immature	Roe up to two years	
		Red/Fallow/Sika up to three years	60 per cent
ii	Mature	Roe three–six years	
		Red/Fallow/Sika four–nine years	20 per cent
			(weaker animals)
iii	Aged	Roe six+ years	
		Red/Fallow/Sika ten+ years	20 per cent

Further selection for trophy quality is possible by the removal of inferior heads before full maturity (about ten years for red deer, somewhat earlier for fallow and sika). The quality of roe antlers, grown in winter, depends too much on nutrition for selective culling to be worthwhile.

With females any attempt at ultra-refined selection is likely to be counter-productive. Cull targets will not be achieved and overstocking results. Some general guidelines for the culling of females should be followed within the general age classes shown above:

i Hinds/does of the larger species with young at heel should not be shot during November/December, when some young are still suckling.

ii After December, if a hind/doe has a female calf/fawn at heel the calf/fawn should be shot first. The hind/doe would be able to survive without its young but the young would probably starve without its parent. An exception to this rule may be made if it is imperative to reduce the stock of breeding females.

iii With red/fallow/sika, who have a matriarchal social system, lead hinds/does should not be shot as this tends to split up and scatter female herds. An exception to this rule may be made if it is necessary to stop them raiding fields, etc.

iv With hill red hinds which often only produce a calf every second year it is advisable to avoid shooting mature, yeld hinds (those without calves). These are the hinds most likely to survive the winter and produce a strong calf the following summer.

Summary

An attempt has been made to provide a very general outline of deer management. With a complex subject covering the four main species, all ranging over widely differing terrains, it is only possible to cover broad principles. *One principle is paramount, that overstocking and underculling (particularly of females) will have disastrous consequences both to the deer and to outside interests.* A stock which has been overculled can build up in a few years. A stock which is underculled may take many years to bring to a proper level.

19

Deer and the Law

The following sections only summarise briefly the main provisions of the law relating to deer and to the permitted methods of taking and killing deer in England and Wales. They are intended as a general guide for the stalker not as an authoritative statement of the law. For legal purposes and detailed provisions, reference should be made to the relevant Acts themselves.

The law in England and Wales differs from the law in Scotland, which is described in the second section.

The Law Relating to Deer in England and Wales

The principle Acts affecting deer in England and Wales are:
 Deer Act 1963
 Firearms Act 1968
 Deer Act 1980
 Wildlife and Countryside Act 1981, schedule 7

Ownership of Deer There is only a limited ownership in wild deer while they are alive, and they cannot be the subject of theft. But when dead, the carcass is the property of the owner or occupier of, or the person having the right to kill deer on, the land where the carcass is lying. Deer which have been lawfully tamed or reclaimed or which are ordinarily kept in captivity, e.g. in a park, deer farm or zoo, are considered to be property unless they regain their natural liberty, and can be the subject of theft.

Methods of Taking or Killing Deer other than by Shooting The setting of any trap, net, snare or poisoned or stupefying bait to take, kill or injure deer is an offence, as is the use of any arrow, spear or similar missile or a missile containing any poison or stupefying drug.

Who may Shoot Deer? Subject to the general provisions of the law and to the possession of the necessary licences and certificates, only the following may, in general terms, shoot deer:

i owners of land who have not disposed of their right to take or kill deer on their land;

ii tenants whose tenancy agreements include the right to take or kill deer on their tenanted land, either as a specific right or as part of general shooting rights;

iii persons who, by agreement with the owner or tenant, have the right to take or kill deer on specified land, either as a specific right or as part of general shooting rights – lessees of shooting rights, for example; the owner or tenant must, of course, have the right to enter into any such agreement;

iv persons authorized (preferably in writing) by a person in category iii above who must, himself, have the right to authorize others.

It is important to remember that the right to shoot deer is often excluded from the general shooting ('sporting') rights.

Firearms Generally a rifle is the only permissible weapon for shooting deer, although the law allows the use of certain shotguns and shotgun ammunition in some circumstances. Any air gun, air rifle and air pistol is prohibited.

Rifles Rifles must have a minimum calibre of 0.240ins (6mm) and a minimum muzzle energy of 1,700ft/lbs (2,305 joules[1]). Ammunition must be designed to expand on impact.

Shotguns If a shotgun is used it must have a minimum gauge of 12 bore and must be loaded with a cartridge containing shot each of which has a diameter of 0.203ins (5.16mm) (AAA) or containing a single non-spherical projectile weighing not less than 350 grains (22.68 grammes) (rifled slug or Brenneke).

Firearm and Shotgun Certificates A firearm certificate is necessary to buy, possess or use the type of rifle and ammunition permissible for shooting

1. One joule (the international unit of energy) = 0.738ft/lbs.

deer and also to buy, possess or use rifled slugs for use in shotguns. Application must be made to the Chief Officer of Police for the area in which the applicant lives. The applicant will be asked to state the purpose for which the rifle is required and where it will be used. Some police forces impose a 'territorial restriction' and issue a certificate available only for a specified area (or areas). The police are entitled to see and satisfy themselves that rifles and ammunition are kept in a safe and secure place when not in use. To buy, possess or use a shotgun, a shotgun certificate must be obtained by application to the police (see page 24 '*Shotguns*').

Restrictions on Carrying a Firearm in a Public Place This is a difficult part of the law for the stalker. He may not carry a rifle (loaded or not) together with ammunition for that rifle in a public place 'without lawful authority or reasonable excuse'. In general, to transport a rifle and ammunition in a vehicle, the rifle being in a case or sleeve and unloaded, to or from the ground on which the stalker has a legal right to stalk should not involve any infringement of the law. The stalker is advised always to carry his firearm certificate with him when out with his rifle, however inconvenient.

Game Licences For all practical purposes a game licence is required for shooting deer. The main exception to this is the killing of deer on enclosed land by the owner or occupier of that land or with his permission.

Close Seasons There are close seasons for most species of deer. These are given on page 159. It is, of course, an offence to take or kill deer during the close seasons, but there are some exceptions.

Exceptions to the Close Seasons Provisions It is not an offence to kill deer by means of shooting during the close seasons in the following circumstances:

i to prevent suffering by an injured or diseased deer;
ii to comply with a direction by the Minister of Agriculture in connection with the prevention of damage by pests;
iii where the shooting is carried out on cultivated land, pasture or enclosed woodland by the occupier of that land, or by his family or employees acting with his written authority;
iv where the shooting is carried out on cultivated land, pasture or enclosed woodland by a person having the right to kill deer on that land or by some other person acting with his written authority.

In iii and iv above, the person shooting the deer must be able to show that he had reasonable grounds for believing that deer of the same species were causing damage and that it was likely that further serious damage would be caused if the deer were not shot.

Shooting at Night (Nightly Close Time) It is an offence to take or kill deer at night i.e. one hour after sunset until one hour before sunrise, unless the animal is seriously injured or diseased.

Use of Vehicles Deer may not be shot from any mechanically propelled vehicle (or aircraft) nor may a vehicle (or aircraft) be used for the purpose of driving deer, except by, or with the written authority of, the occupier of the enclosed land where the deer are usually kept.

Sale of Venison Unless you are a licensed game dealer, you may not sell any venison to anyone except a licensed game dealer, nor may you sell any venison to anyone during the 'prohibited period' (i.e. the period commencing with the tenth day of the close season for that species and sex of deer and ending with the end of that close season). It is also an offence for anyone to sell, purchase or receive any venison which he has reason to believe has come from a deer killed illegally. Licensed game dealers are required to keep records giving details of all venison purchased, including particulars of the seller.

Poaching

i It is an offence to enter any land without lawful authority in search or pursuit of any deer.
ii It is an offence for any person, while on any land, intentionally to take, kill or injure any deer without lawful authority.
iii It is also an offence for any person, while on any land, to remove the carcass of any deer without lawful authority.

If he suspects that an offence is being or has been committed under i, ii or iii above, an authorized person (i.e. a police officer, the owner or occupier of the land, any person authorized by him, and any person having the right to kill deer on that land) has the right to require the suspect to give his full name and address and to quit the land forthwith. Failure to comply with either request is a serious offence.

Powers of the Police Where they suspect that a person is committing or has committed an offence under the Deer Acts, the police are empowered, without warrant, to stop and search that person and to search or examine any vehicle, animal, weapon or other thing which they believe may provide evidence of the offence. In addition, they have power to seize and detain the evidence and to arrest a suspect who fails to give his full name and address.

Penalties Offences under the Deer Acts carry penalties, on conviction, of fines of up to £500 or imprisonment for three months or both. The fine may be imposed in respect of each deer involved in the offence.

In addition, the court may order the confiscation of any deer in respect of which the offence was committed, and any vehicle, animal, weapon or other thing which was capable of being used to take, kill or injure deer and which was found in the offender's possession.

The court may also disqualify an offender from holding a game dealer's licence and, in certain circumstances, cancel any firearm or shotgun certificate.

The Law Relating to Deer in Scotland

The principle Acts affecting deer in Scotland are:
  Deer (Scotland) Act 1959
  Firearms Act 1968
  Deer (Amendment) (Scotland) Act 1982

Ownership of Deer The position in Scotland is substantially the same as it is in England and Wales.

Conservation and Control One of the main differences between the deer laws of Scotland and those in force in England and Wales is that in Scotland under the 1959 Act a body known as the Red Deer Commission was set up. The Commission (RDC) has the general function of 'furthering the conservation and control of red deer and of keeping under review all matters relating to red deer'. It has particular powers to deal with marauding deer. The Commission's powers were extended by the 1982 Act to cover other species in certain circumstances. No similar body exists in England and Wales.

Methods of Killing Deer In Scotland it is an offence to kill deer otherwise than by shooting; that is, by the use of a permitted firearm. No other method is permissible except to prevent suffering by an injured or diseased deer or by an orphaned calf, fawn or kid.

Who may Shoot Deer? The paragraph outlining the position in England and Wales applies largely to Scotland.

Firearms The 1959 Act as amended provides that the Secretary of State shall have power to make such Order as he thinks fit regarding the classes of firearms, ammunition, sights and other equipment which may lawfully be used in connection with the killing of deer. Although the amending Act came into force on 28 July 1982 no such Order has yet been promulgated.

Firearm and Shotgun Certificates, Carrying Firearms in a Public Place, Game Licences The position in Scotland is, in general, similar to that in England and Wales. A game licence is not required for killing deer in certain circumstances under a requirement or authorization by the RDC.

Close seasons It is an offence to take, kill or injure deer during the close seasons (see page 159).

Exceptions to the Close Seasons Provisions It is not an offence to take or kill deer during the close seasons in the following circumstances:
   i   to prevent suffering by an injured or diseased deer or an orphaned calf, fawn or kid;
   ii where the act is done under the authority of or at the request of the RDC;
   iii on a deer farm enclosed by a deer-proof barrier, where the deer are conspicuously marked;
   iv where the occupier of enclosed agricultural land or enclosed woodland has reasonable grounds for believing that serious damage will be caused to crops, pasture, trees or foodstuffs on that land if the deer are not killed, and where the shooting is carried out by
   a   the owner in person[1]
   b   the owner's servants[1]
   c   the occupier in person

   1. Each of these categories requires the written authorization of the occupier.

d the occupier's servants[1]
e other persons normally resident on the land[1]
f any other person approved in writing by the RDC as a fit and
   competent person[1].

Shooting at Night This is generally forbidden except that the occupier of agricultural land or enclosed woodland may, in person, shoot red or sika deer at night i.e. one hour after sunset until one hour before sunrise, provided that he has reasonable grounds for believing that serious damage will be caused to crops, pasture, trees or foodstuffs on that land if the deer are not killed. Also, subject to certain exacting criteria, the RDC may authorize any person, nominated by the occupier, to shoot deer of any species at night. The RDC have issued a Code of Practice for shooting deer at night.

Use of Vehicles Deer may not be shot from an aircraft, nor may a vehicle be used for the purpose of driving deer on unenclosed land with the intention of taking, killing or injuring them. Live deer may not be transported by air except inside the aircraft. ('Vehicle' includes an aircraft and 'aircraft' includes a helicopter.)

Sale of Venison No one, unless he is a licensed venison dealer, may sell any venison to anyone except a licensed venison dealer unless he has bought it from a licensed venison dealer. Further, it is an offence for anyone to sell, purchase or receive any venison from a deer which he has reason to believe has been killed unlawfully. Licensed venison dealers must keep detailed records of all transactions in venison.

Poaching It is an offence for any person to take, kill or injure deer on any land without legal right.
   It is an offence for any person to remove the carcass of a deer from any land without legal right.

Powers of the Police Apart from his powers under Common Law, a police officer may seize any deer, firearm or ammunition, vehicle or boat which is liable to be forfeited on conviction of an offence under the 1959 Act as amended. In addition to extensive powers under other legislation the police, where they suspect certain, specified offences under the Act, may also, by reason of urgency, stop, search and seize without warrant any vehicle or boat which may provide evidence of the offence. And they may arrest any person found committing any of these specified offences.

Penalties Conviction of the more serious offences under the Act carries penalties of a maximum fine of £500 for each deer in respect of which the offence was committed or up to three months imprisonment or both.

Where two or more persons act together, each is liable to considerably increased penalties.

There are also provisions for the forfeiture of illegally killed deer, firearms, equipment and vehicles, for the cancellation of firearm and shotgun certificates, and for the revocation of venison dealers' licences.

20

Ways of Stalking Deer

Different stalking techniques are required for the two very different types of terrain in which British deer are found: the largely treeless hill and mountain areas of the Scottish Highlands, and the woods and forests of lowland Britain.

Highland stalking presents fewer problems to the beginner, escorted by a professional stalker who guides him and selects the deer to be shot. The wise novice must not only obey the stalker's instructions: he can learn a great deal by observing and listening to him.

An essential condition for most Highland stalking is physical fitness. In a day's stalking the 'Rifle' (the Scottish term for the hunter, to distinguish him from the 'stalker', the professional), may climb 2,000–3,000ft (600–900m) and walk anything from 5–20 miles(8–32km), most of it over very difficult country.

On the open hill deer can be seen at considerable distances, often of several miles. The stalking party is equally visible to the deer and must utilize what cover is provided by the ground, frequently crawling the last few hundred yards of a stalk. Most shots are taken from the prone position, possibly with the left hand (*not* the rifle) resting on a tussock or stone. Highland deer are often shot at longer ranges than is the case in woodland stalking, most shots being taken between 100–200yds(90–180m).

It is essential that the Rifle should be familiar with the weapon he is to use and that he has fired and zeroed it himself before attempting to shoot at a deer. He must shoot only at the beast which the stalker indicates and wait until the animal presents a broadside view providing a heart or lung shot. (He must ensure that he knows where these are – see Figure 10.) Before firing he should see that there is nothing, even including grass or

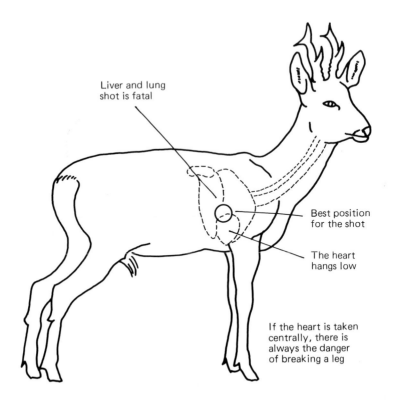

Liver and lung
shot is fatal

Best position
for the shot

The heart
hangs low

If the heart is taken
centrally, there is
always the danger
of breaking a leg

Figure 10 *Broadside view showing the most vulnerable areas*

heather, which could deflect the bullet. After firing he should reload immediately in case a second shot is needed.

The beginner in the Highlands has a further advantage as the professional stalker will 'gralloch' (that is eviscerate) the stag. The beginner should observe carefully how this is done with the object of learning how to do it himself.

In woodland stalking the beginner has more to learn because he is much more on his own. No one should begin without accompanying an experienced stalker on numerous occasions, observing what he does, asking questions and receiving advice.

Basically, there are two methods of stalking in woodland: sitting and waiting for the deer, or walking round looking for them.

'Sitting up' involves either the use of a roughly constructed hide overlooking a field or clearing, or a 'high seat'. These are platforms constructed in a tree and reached by a ladder, holding one, or sometimes

Stalkers on the hill with binoculars and the more traditional telescope. Spying is a great part of the day's enjoyment

Hill ponies at Inchnadamph are still used on some deer forests to carry the stags down to the vehicles

| a | b Arley junior | c Arley lean-to against tree | d Forestry Commission 'Alice Holt' |

Figure 11 *High seats*
   a) A platform constructed in a tree, access by ladder
   b) A steel manufactured, free-standing version
   c) Again a steel manufactured version, this time supported by a tree
   d) Larger metal model used by the Forestry Commission

two, stalkers.[1] High seats can also be made free-standing on locations where there are no convenient trees (see Figure 11). The height of the seat from the ground depends upon the present – and future – height of the surrounding cover.

Sitting up in a high seat is generally a more productive method than moving about the wood and offers several advantages. Firstly, the stalker, being well above ground, is much less likely to be scented by deer and, provided he sits still and quietly, is less likely to be seen or heard. Deer rarely look up. Secondly, if the high seat is well sited he should have a fairly extensive field of view enabling him to study the deer and shoot selectively. Thirdly, he has a rail on which to rest his hand when firing. Fourthly, a most important point, firing downwards from a high seat is much safer than shooting on level ground as the bullet grounds itself immediately.

Though offering fewer advantages than a high seat, the hide is cheaper to construct and can be used for short periods in locations where a high seat would be unjustified.

Otherwise, the stalker moves through the forest as quietly as he can,

---

1. Note the different use of the word 'stalker' in England and Wales, from Scotland; see also Glossary.

taking great care to move into whatever wind there may be, or at worst to have it blowing from one side, never from behind. Unfortunately, wind in woodland often eddies and the stalker must be prepared for sudden turbulence, especially at junctions of rides.

Movement must be slow with frequent halts during which the undergrowth ahead, and on both sides, is studied through the binoculars. Most deer stop just within the cover on the sides of a ride and look and listen before emerging; these are the occasions when careful scrutiny may disclose a twitching ear or a moving head.

The stalker must be neither scented, heard nor seen, because alerted deer give no opportunity for a careful, selective and deliberate shot. 'Snap' shots at startled and rapidly departing deer must *never* be attempted.

Shots taken when moving through the forest are normally fired from the standing position or, occasionally, sitting. In both cases the stalker is recommended to use a stout stick to steady the left hand (for right-handed stalkers). The stick should be stiff enough not to be 'whippy' and be about the same height as the stalker. When taking a shot the forward end of the rifle stock is held lightly in, or resting on, the hand holding the stick. Although this does not prevent sideways 'wobble' it should prevent any movement up and down.

When stalking on foot and shooting from ground level the stalker must consider the background beyond his target. This must be adequate to stop a bullet. An earth bank or the side of a ravine is ideal; a thick plantation, especially of young timber, is also excellent. If there is any doubt about the effectiveness of the background to stop or break up a bullet *the shot must not be taken.*

Most woodland deer are shot at comparatively short ranges, 50–100yds (45–90m) being typical. Because deer usually move only at dawn and dusk shooting in dense woodland is often in very poor light; consequently, a telescopic sight with good light-gathering properties is essential.

The beginner must either have his deer selected by the stalker organizing the cull or, if without such help, must make his own management plan, shooting only deer which conform to the culling plan in sex, age and condition and, of course, conforming to the legal open seasons; see page 159.

The novice should shoot only at deer which are broadside on, aiming for a heart or lung shot. He must know where these are in all deer (see Figure 10, page 174).

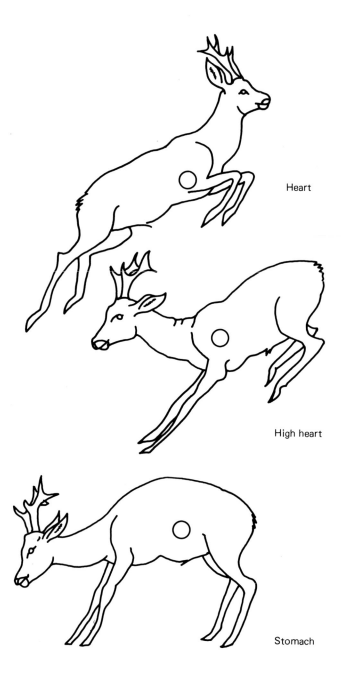

Heart

High heart

Stomach

Figure 12 *Reaction to shot*

Shot deer very rarely fall where they stand and in woodland have only a few yards to move to be in cover. A heart-shot beast may run 50 yards or more before dropping and finding it may be a problem. The stalker should put his hat or some other visible object where he took the shot and then go to where the deer was standing, having marked this spot when taking the shot, by some adjacent feature. The ground and vegetation should be carefully examined for traces of blood, cut hair, or even flesh or bone. When a high-velocity small-calibre rifle is used, however, there may well be none; see Figure 12 and chapter twenty-three 'Firearms for Deer' for further details.

A dog trained to follow wounded deer on a lead is invaluable, provided the cover is not too thick. In dense cover a dog who will bay a wounded deer or bark on finding a dead one is a pearl beyond price, but rare! Almost any dog is better than none, but without one the stalker must rely on his eyes; hands brushed through the grass and undergrowth may disclose otherwise invisible blood. It is generally wise to wait at least fifteen minutes before following a shot deer into cover to give a hard-hit beast time to expire or, at any rate, stiffen up before being approached.

Deer may also be brought to the rifle by calling them during the rut. This method works only with red, roe and sika as fallow do not respond. Widely used on the Continent, calling in Great Britain is unpredictable in its results. Numerous roe calls are marketed. Practice and experiment are essential for even modest success.

The woodland stalker must gralloch his own deer; this should be done as soon as possible after shooting. If the journey to base is a short one it may be best to do this at home to keep the carcass clean. The technique must be learned from an experienced stalker and first attempted under supervision.

The Stalker's Code[1]

All stalkers – whether woodland 'stalkers' in the Lowlands or 'Rifles' in the Highlands – must observe the Stalker's Code.

The stalker's behaviour should be guided by respect:

For the deer and all wildlife
For the land, forests and crops
For the people who work in the countryside, and
For everyone who enjoys our woods and hills and fields.

1. Issued by the General Council of the British Deer Society.

He should conform to these simple rules:

Study firearms safety at all times: nothing is more important.

Be considerate: greed or selfishness spoils everything – for you and for other people.

Conserve deer resources: do not over-exploit them.

Obey the law: particularly on weapons, on seasons, and on where you stalk.

Learn all you can about deer: shooting should not be all-important.

Identify your target for certain before lifting the rifle.

Shoot calmly: avoid any shot likely to wound – above all at a distant, moving or dimly seen deer.

If possible keep and train a dog to follow up the shot.

Observe the letter and the spirit of the Country Code (available from the Countryside Commission, Crescent Place, Cheltenham).

21

Converting a Deer Carcass into Venison[1]

Having made a clean shot, the stalker's aim should be to make the very best use of the deer. The meat should be kept scrupulously clean and nothing wasted which can be used.

Having made sure that the animal is dead, it is laid on its back and an incision made by pinching up the skin of the belly on the centre line and cutting with the knife held sideways so that the point does not enter the stomach. Two fingers are inserted in this cut with the knife point between them and thus the incision is continued backwards to the vent and forwards to the ribs.

With male deer the external genitalia are freed backwards to the vent but not cut away. By cutting carefully round the vent, these and the end of the gut can be pushed forward through the pelvis and they then come away with the rest of the intestines without risk of contaminating the meat with urine.

The ribs are then cut along the line of the sternum, in the case of a young beast using the knife-blade or for an older one the saw. The windpipe and gullet are exposed and freed from the neck and cut off below the head. These are pulled back and progressively freed from the body cavity. The diaphragm is cut close to the ribs, first on the one side and then on the other, and the whole of the body contents can be lifted out.

Evidence of the placing of the shot and its effect on the tissues can be studied at this point. The liver is inspected for evidence of disease and, if healthy, should be put with the kidneys and the heart in a polythene bag

1. This chapter was originally published in Richard Prior's *Roe Deer: Management and Stalking,* (Game Conservancy), to whom grateful acknowledgement is made.

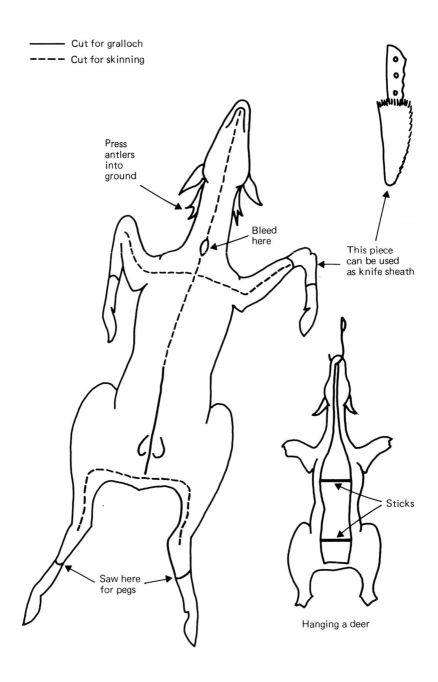

Cut for gralloch
Cut for skinning

Press
antlers
into
ground

Bleed
here

This piece
can be used
as knife sheath

Sticks

Saw here
for pegs

Hanging a deer

Figure 13 *Gralloching and skinning*

for human consumption. The stomach should be emptied of its contents and put in another polythene bag with the lungs for dog food. The rest of the body contents must be buried or at least hidden well away from any paths. The carcass is hung up to drain or turned on its front with its legs spread out if flies are troublesome.

Skinning is easiest done when the carcass is still warm, but venison dries quickly when exposed to the air, after a time forming a hard, dark skin. It is better to delay skinning until the meat is ready to eat. In summer this may be as soon as twenty-four hours while, in winter, a carcass can hang to advantage for seven to eight days.

Start skinning by making cuts along the inside of the legs to join up with the central incision, then ease away the skin from the hock joints so that the animal may be suspended by hooks through the ham-strings. A low beam in which two staples can be fixed about 30ins(760mm) apart is ideal for skinning. A stout hook from these to each hind leg will hold the animal suspended for skinning without it twisting as you work.

Hang it up and pull the skin from the meat, working always from the belly incision towards the backbone, or the meat will tear. Much can be done by pulling, using the knife as little as possible. Great care must be taken to avoid the meat getting covered with loose hairs. If the stomach was ruptured by the shot any areas of green-stained meat must be cut away otherwise the carcass will not keep.

The head can now be cut off close behind the ears, either using a saw or by disconnecting the vertebrae. It should not be left attached to a skinned carcass because parasites may emerge from the hair and be discovered adhering to the meat. Disjoint and cut off the lower limbs.

To cut the carcass into joints, hang it from the two hooks and remove the shoulders by cutting the muscles between foreleg and ribs and gently pulling outwards. There is no bone to cut. Lay the joints on a clean plastic sheet. Then, using the saw, take the ribs off just clean of the fillet and divide the two haunches as far as the loin but no farther. Sever the backbone at the tenth rib counting forward, so that the neck comes away. This section can be boned, using the meat for a stew and the bones for stock. Cut the backbone again just in front of the haunches which detaches the saddle and leaves two haunches hanging up.

22

The Stalker's Equipment

The most essential equipment for the stalker is, of course, his rifle and ammunition, described in chapter twenty-three, 'Firearms for Deer'. The stalker will also require the following:

Clothing The Highland deer stalker requires rather different clothing from the woodland stalker. In the Highlands, tweeds of a neutral shade and quiet pattern are most suitable; very light or dark shades should be avoided. Breeches may be a little fuller round the knee than is necessary in lowland stalking. Hats or caps should be low in the crown and fit well. Boots or shoes should be rubber-soled and well cleated for grip. The coat should have large pockets in which to carry an additional woolly pullover, a light (camouflaged) waterproof, sandwiches and a flask. Alternatively, a light haversack could be used.

The woodland stalker is best dressed in predominantly green or brown shades; a camouflage smock is useful; breeches or trousers of corduroy or loden cloth. A hat or cap with a good brim to shade the face is essential. Boots or shoes should be rubber-soled and well cleated. Nylon or stiff waterproof outer clothing should be avoided as it is noisy. Deer have monochromatic but very acute vision; texture is more important than colour.

Binoculars and Telescopes In the Highlands a telescope is necessary because of the distances to be spied. The professional stalker will usually carry one. The Rifle may carry binoculars but they can be a nuisance when crawling.

In woodland binoculars are essential. Good light-gathering power is more important than high magnification; 7 × 50 is probably the most widely used binocular.

Stick If used in the Highlands this will be as an aid to walking and to steady the telescope. In woodland – as we have explained earlier – it will be used for taking a shot when stalking; well-seasoned hazel about the height of the stalker will be suitable for the purpose.

Knife The Highland novice may not need one since the professional stalker will 'gralloch' the deer, but the woodland stalker must *never* be without a suitable knife.

Knives can be of either fixed- or folding-blade design; if the latter, the main blade must *lock* when open. An additional blade with a 'hooded' tip is very useful for gralloching. Many stalking knives incorporate a bone saw. A small sharpening stone in a case is also useful.

Insect Repellant and/or Smoking Materials If stalking when biting insects are numerous, remember that violent movement of the hands and arms to destroy marauders is a good way of repelling deer as well; protection against biting insects is advisable.

23

Firearms for Deer

Rifles

Actions

There are six main types of action, for centre-fire cartridges, available for shooting deer:

Single or double-barrelled action	Single shot only from each barrel or rifle/shotgun combinations
Falling-block action	Single shot only
Under-lever action	Magazine repeater
Pump or slide action	Magazine repeater
Semi-automatic action	Magazine repeater
Turn-bolt action	Either single shot or magazine repeaters

The turn-bolt type of actioned rifle is the one most used by stalkers and the Mauser pattern has been most generally followed.

Permissible Firearms

The only really effective and humane weapon for shooting deer is a rifle as defined in the Deer Act 1963 (England and Wales). Owing to imperfections in the law, other firearms can be used in England and Wales and an even wider variety in Scotland. These are quite unsuitable, causing more wounding than killing.

Calibre, Ballistics: Bullet Weight and Muzzle Velocity

A simple definition of 'the best deer cartridge' is impossible.

As a guide, pointed or spitzer-shaped bullets are ideally suited for deer, but circumstances alter their acceptability. On open ground deer are usually shot at longer ranges than in woodland and it is for these greater distances that the pointed bullet from the smaller calibre rifles, with their higher velocities and flatter trajectories, are best suited, while the round soft-nosed bullet comes into its own at the shorter ranges found in woodland stalking where high velocities and flat trajectories are less necessary. But remember that all bullets deviate from their true paths on contact with vegetation and, the lighter the bullet, the more it will depart from the target. Some of the higher velocity rounds may break up if they touch a twig.

The stalker choosing a deer rifle should look at the range of calibres from .243ins(6mm) to .323ins(8mm) as the selection of suitable bullet weights for deer commences at 100 grains and rises to 250 grains; he should consider these in relation to the species of deer he is likely to hunt.

A stalker might consider owning two rifles as there is no such thing as an 'all-round weapon' (and there is always the unforeseen situation where one rifle is out of commission), but much flexibility can be achieved by varying the weight of bullet used.

The list of stalking rifles and bullet weights that follows is not intended to be comprehensive, but merely to show the beginner some of the more widely used calibres. The rifles listed are primarily bolt-action magazine rifles, but several are available in other constructions such as double-barrelled rifles; under-lever; single-shot; or in rifle/shotgun combination actions. Bullet construction is not discussed in the following lists, although there is a very wide variety of bullet types. All bullets for use on deer are designed to expand on impact.

There is no standard method of describing rifle calibres and cartridges. English and American practice is generally to describe the calibre by decimal fractions of an inch, e.g. .243ins, but this becomes confusing when the date of first manufacture is added, as in the .30-06, that is, .30ins calibre, first manufactured in 1906. The calibre is only one factor in rifle cartridge description; of equal importance is the case length.

For this reason the Continental method of describing rifle cartridges is both more logical and informative. The first figure given is the calibre, the second the case length, e.g., 7 × 57 – both measurements in millimetres. The importance of this can be seen when it is realized that there are at least seven 7mm cartridges, no two of which are interchangeable.

In the following list examples of both forms of description are given. Before buying any rifle the beginner should ensure that ammunition is readily available and will continue to be manufactured.

Calibre	*Commonly Used Bullet Weights*
.243″ Win (Winchester)	100 grains (gr.) A suitable rifle and round for roe but rather light for anything larger.
.256″	This is made in a considerable number of cartridge lengths ranging from the 6.5 × 54mm to a powerful magnum 6.5 × 68mm. Probably the most widely used in Great Britain is the .256 Mannlicher Schonauer firing a 160 gr. bullet. Considered old-fashioned by some it is, nevertheless, a good roe rifle.
.270″ Win	A fine American round. The 130 gr. bullet at 3,140ft(957m)/sec. muzzle velocity is suitable for stalking in open conditions, whilst the 150 gr. at 2,800ft(853m)/sec. is more suitable for woodland stalking.
7 × 57mm	One of the older but most widely used deer rifles. A wide range of bullet weights, of which the 150 gr. is probably the most useful. Ideal for woodland stalking and less recoil than most.
7 mm Rem. Magnum	A very powerful rifle available with bullet weights ranging from 140 to 175 gr.
.30-06 Springfield	Probably the most widely used sporting-rifle cartridge in the world. This is the great, time-honoured cartridge by which all others are measured. If an all-round cartridge exists, this may well be it.
	Bullet weights range from 110 gr. with a muzzle velocity of 3,370ft(1,027m)/sec. to 220 gr. at 2,410ft(735m)/sec. Probably the most generally useful round for deer is the 150 gr. at 2,970 ft(905m)/sec.
.303″ British	The standard British service calibre until after World War II. Used worldwide in the days of the Empire. The 150 gr. bullet at 2,720ft(825m)/sec is perfectly adequate for all British deer and a converted .303 sporter is one of the cheapest rifles to buy.

.308″ Win (the 7.62 × 51mm NATO round adapted to sporting purposes)	Bullet weights range from 110 gr. at 3,340ft(1018m)/sec to 200 gr. at 2,450ft(747m)/sec. A popular calibre; ammunition readily available.
8 × 57mm	In Europe probably the most widely used calibre, but now gradually being supplanted by more modern rounds such as the 7 × 64mm. (Note: The J and S versions of the 8 × 57mm cartridge are *not* interchangeable. S rounds should only be used in rifles marked JS or JSR.)

NOTE: Although muzzle velocity is used above to indicate the relative performance of different rounds, it should not be looked upon as the most important measure of effectiveness or killing power. No one measurement can be used for this, as many factors make up the 'best round' for the job. Having said this, the most widely used single indicator of performance is striking energy at 100 yards (or metres), measured in ft/lbs.

Shotguns

While it is legal to use shotguns only in very limited and specific circumstances, their use must conform to the law which, in England and Wales, lays down a minimum of 12-bore and a minimum of 0.203ins (5mm) diameter for the shot contained in a 12-bore cartridge, e.g., AAA or larger, or rifled slug.

Using this type of load, accuracy is limited as the number of shot is such that the pattern is poor and, should the hapless deer be struck by a few pellets, the energy is barely sufficient to penetrate the brain or heart to kill it at anything but point-blank range, under 20yds(18m).

If a shotgun must be used, which is deplorable, the cartridge selected should be that loaded with a single projectile and known as rifled or brenneke slug; this is only obtainable with a Firearm Certificate. The gun should, preferably, be single-barrelled and fitted with a proper foresight and rearsight, when groups of 4–8ins(102–203mm) at 50yds(46m) can be expected, fired from a bench. The use of this weapon should be restricted to a range of under 50 yards. Use of a double-barrelled shotgun with rifled slug or similar cartridge is less desirable, as acceptable accuracy is less easy to achieve. *Rifled slugs can ricochet freely.* It is also imperative *not* to use ammunition of 2¾ins(70mm) manufacture in a shotgun chambered only for 2½ins(64mm).

Zeroing

A rifle with only open sights is an exception nowadays as the telescopic sight has been so developed that the better quality products are virtually weather- and foolproof; they are not proof, however, against the incompetent stalker who has never heard of the care of arms.

If a stalker has a telescopic sight fitted it is obligatory to check the zero of his rifle by firing a minimum of three rounds for a group, especially if he uses that rifle only half a dozen times a year. The zeroing must be carried out in a completely safe location. The following points will assist those wishing to zero their rifles which may lose accuracy for such reasons as the warping of the stock, or the rifle or sight being dropped or knocked, or many other reasons.

  i Check and tighten all stock-bedding screws and all screws which retain the blocks and rings which secure the telescopic sight to the receiver of the rifle.

 ii Bore-sight the rifle. Remove the bolt. Place the fore-end of the rifle on a sandbagged bench rest; also place toe of butt on a similar support. Look through sight at the target and, holding the rifle steady, check the target through the barrel, as if using a peep sight. If the picture through the sight and barrel appears to be central, only minor adjustment should be required. But, if the view through the barrel shows the target off-centre, larger adjustments will be required.

iii Minor corrections are achieved by using the elevation or windage-adjustment turrets on the body of the telescopic sight, using the turret situated on top to correct errors in elevation (up or down) and the turret found on the right-hand side to rectify errors in windage (left or right).

Most modern telescopic sights are as described above but, if other constructions are encountered, the advice of a gunsmith specializing in rifles should be sought.

On removing the dust-covers from each turret, a large milled and slotted screw, or sometimes a milled knob, is exposed, showing on the elevation screw or knob the word 'UP' and an arrow which usually points to the right or clockwise direction; if moved in this direction it will move the bullet impact higher on the target. The screw is graduated in minutes which represent approximately 1in(25mm) at 100 yards or metres. One minute of movement is usually achieved in either two or four distinct and audible clicks which, in theory, should move the impact of the bullet

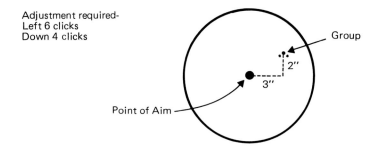

Adjustment required-
Left 6 clicks
Down 4 clicks

Group

2"

3"

Point of Aim

Example: Sight graduated at 2 clicks = 1 minute of angle (e.g. 1" at 100 yards)

Figure 14 *Zeroing – telescopic sight correction*

either $\frac{1}{2}$in(12.5mm) or $\frac{1}{4}$in according to the sight used. The windage screw or knob operates in a similar manner, save that the letter 'L' and an arrow pointing anti-clockwise is shown and, if moved in this direction, will move the bullet impact to the left (see Figure 14).

If any adjustment other than a minor correction is required it is best to ask a skilled person to make the adjustments necessary.

When zeroing a rifle it is wise to make an adjustment only after firing three rounds. Judge the centre of the group and move the sight in the direction required; otherwise, if you correct after every shot, you chase the error over the target and this can prove costly in the consumption of ammunition. The first group should be fired at a range of 25 yards, as errors are minimized at this range; unless the error is large the bullets should be somewhere on the target. When corrections have been made and the rifle is consistently grouping in the desired place at 25 yards, further groups should be fired at 100 yards to confirm grouping consistency at actual stalking ranges.

Don't be proud! Use a firm and suitable rest when zeroing your rifle. Much ammunition will otherwise be wasted!

Shooting Skill and Safety

One can never become the perfect rifleman, but practice can make the average shot into a marksman. Obviously the stalker who uses his rifle half-a-dozen times a year and fires perhaps one or two boxes of cartridges has not the ability of another who fires many hundreds of rounds of centre-fire ammunition on rifle ranges, for this practice inspires confidence in one's ability to hit a target and develops familiarity with the rifle until it becomes an extension of one's arms and a part of one's body. Even ten minutes a day spent in handling the rifle and doing 'shoot to kill' exercises at dummy targets on a wall will provide the essential familiarity.

Bolts must be removed from rifles when in the home. This serves two purposes: the weapon is entirely safe for practice handling and, of course, with the bolt locked away elsewhere the rifle is useless if stolen.

Actions should always be kept open when going to, or returning from, a rifle range. The only time the action is closed and a cartridge chambered is when about to fire at a target on the range or at the commencement of stalking.

If there should be a delay, for whatever reason, in firing on the range, *immediately* open the action and eject the chambered round; when the rifle is loaded for stalking it *must* be carried with the safety catch applied. The catch should only be released just prior to firing at a deer.

The great axiom of safety, which should be indelibly burned into the mind of everyone who handles a firearm, is *never, never* point it at anything living unless it is to be used in earnest. Always treat a firearm as *loaded* until you have proved otherwise.

Safe Handling and Carrying a Rifle

On reaching the stalking area load the rifle with four rounds (for a magazine with a capacity of five cartridges), close the bolt and *ensure* that a cartridge is chambered; then apply the safety catch. By incompletely charging the magazine the spring is not fully compressed under the magazine platform and will give less faulty feeding from the magazine over the years.

Sling the rifle over either shoulder with the muzzle facing forwards and upwards; it is easier to bring the rifle to the aim from this position than if the rifle is conventionally slung behind the shoulder. By keeping the muzzle upwards there is less danger of obstructing the barrel with debris should one fall; but, in rain, the muzzle can be carried downwards or sellotape placed over it.

Firing and Follow-up

The beginner must only take a broadside shot at a standing animal. If the stalker then visualizes an inverted white triangle situated immediately behind the shoulder of a roe deer, pointing downwards and just touching the heart, measuring about 6ins(152mm) along the base line sited below the spine and about 7ins(178mm) to the point which rests on the heart, this is the perfect area in which to place the bullet. The triangle will be proportionately larger in bigger deer. The actions that should follow the shot have already been described in chapter twenty, 'Ways of Stalking Deer', but some further effects are detailed here.

The modern hunting soft-point or hollow-point bullet is so designed and constructed that, on striking the deer, the jacket, usually of copper, is ruptured and begins to peel backwards like a banana, in possibly three or more segments. The soft internal lead flows outwards over the backward-peeling jacket, giving the appearance of a mushroom to the top of the expanded bullet which, when fully expanded, should be two to three times the diameter of the bullet.

The stalker's mental picture should record the reaction of the deer to the shot which gives an indication as to whether the animal was hit and, if so, where the bullet struck (see Figure 12, page 178).

If the deer falls where it stood an alarm bell should ring in the mind and the stalker be prepared to fire again, as it is uncommon for this to happen if the bullet placement was correct.

The reaction of a deer hit in the triangle area is to jump into the air, with fore and aft feet almost coming together, and then to make off at high speed. The noise of the bullet striking in this area is a good heavy thud, but to hear this is exceptional as it is only audible separately from the explosion of the cartridge, at long ranges. If, unfortunately, your bullet hits far back in the stomach area the animal usually drops its head, hunches its back and moves off not quite so fast, giving the appearance of walking on its toes; sometimes it only moves a short distance and allows a second shot. If the stomach wound is not severe, however, the deer will travel a considerable distance and a good dog should be put on to the trail after a lapse of perhaps fifteen or twenty minutes. A bullet striking the stomach makes a dull, sucking plop.

Blood and the coloration of cut hairs give the first clues to where the bullet struck, as darker hairs usually come from the top of the body and lighter ones from the underside. If the blood is frothy and contains lung tissue then the trail to the fallen deer is well signposted and should not be long; but, if there is little or no blood, or blood mixed with stomach contents, it must be assumed that the animal has carried on, wounded in the abdomen, and a long search may be necessary. If there is little blood, with small particles of flesh and curved pieces of bone, then the shot has been placed too low and the animal has a broken leg. The worst possible conditions now exist for the animal and the stalker must immediately follow whatever trail is visible, using a good dog if available.

If there is no apparent reaction to the shot, do not assume a miss: make a meticulous search of the area – on hands and knees if necessary. Only when not one particle of evidence of a hit can be discovered may a miss be assumed.

Two further actions remain. Firstly, the zero of the rifle should be checked and the weapon must not be used again until this has been done, as this may be the reason for the miss. Secondly, the landowner or gamekeeper concerned should be informed so that a watch can be kept on the area for a wounded animal.

Practical Firing on a Range and in the Field

Besides ensuring that his rifle is zeroed, a stalker should fire it on a range and in the field in simulated practical situations.

Practice should be on a life-size roe buck target and, whether on the range or in the field, shots should be fired from the prone, sitting, standing or 'off-hand' positions and using a stick or tree to steady the rifle.

In the prone, sitting or rested positions, groups of three shots at 100 yards or metres should not exceed 4ins(102mm). Standing 'off-hand' or using a tree to steady the rifle, groups of three shots at 100 yards or metres should be within 8ins(203mm).

As a last reminder, never support the rifle directly on any hard object; this may cause the weapon to jump or flip when fired, causing the shot to be off-target. Always place your hand or forearm between the rifle and the object being used as a rest or steadier. If shooting at ranges longer than normal, and when time permits, a rolled-up coat or soft haversack can be used to make an ideal rest.

Acknowledgements

In addition to the authors of the various chapters (listed in the table of contents), I am grateful to a number of other experts who have provided guidance and advice. These include: Dr G.R. Potts, PhD; Mike Street, MSc, MIBiol. (Game Conservancy); G.K. Whitehead (St Hubert Club); W.A. Cadman, BA, OBE; Dr P. Delap, MC; J. Hotchkis (Federation of Deer Control and Management Societies); E. Luxmoore; Ken Topping (Shooting Sports Trust Ltd).

Illustrations have been undertaken by Rodger McPhail and Robert Gillmor.

All photographs provided by John Marchington were kindly donated. Other photographs from: Major G. Carlisle; K.R. Duff and Roy A. Harris; Dr Pamela Harrison; Dave Parfitt; Roy Shaw; and the late John Tarlton.

Figures 1 to 9 in the deer section are published by kind permission of Blackwell Scientific Publications; other diagrams in that section by kind permission of the British Deer Society and the Forestry Commission. Wildfowl photographs by kind permission of Collins Ltd and the British Association for Shooting and Conservation.

Chapter four on 'The Law and Shooting' was kindly commissioned by the British Field Sports Society.

Notes on Contributors

The Editor of this book, Charles Coles, is the former Director of the Game Conservancy. He now acts as Consultant to that organization, and is one of the British representatives on the EEC committee (FACE), dealing with all aspects of game management and conservation throughout the Community. He is the author of several books on shooting and wildlife subjects.

Other contributors to the book include Major the Hon P.C. Baillie, JP; D. Bingham, Editor of *The Field*; Major A.J. Coats; Lt. Col. R.H.A. Cockburn,

Head Ranger Forestry Commission; K.D. Dent; G.T. Garwood MSc, CEng, FICE, FIEE (alias Gough Thomas, Gun Editor of the *Shooting Times*); Major P.A. Gouldsbury, MBE; D. Graham-Hogg; R.E. Green, PhD; G.J.M. Hirons, BSc, D.Phil; P.J. Hudson, BSc, D.Phil; A.J. Knibbs; B. Martin, Assistant Editor, the *Shooting Times*; I. McCall, BSc; R. Prior; R.W. Rayson, St Hubert Club; J. Richards, BA, NDA, MRACDipFM, BASC; J. Swift, MA, MPhil, BASC; S.C. Tapper, PhD; Webley & Scott, National Smallbore Rifle Association, Eley Ammunition Department of IMI Ltd; Lt. Col. C.G. Wright, British Deer Society Stalker Training Committee.

Contributing Organizations

British Association for Shooting and Conservation, Marford Mill, Rossett, Wrexham, Clwyd LL12 0HL

British Deer Society, Mill House, Bishopstrow, Warminster, Wiltshire BA12 9HJ

British Field Sports Society, 59 Kennington Road, London SW1 7PZ

British Shooting Sports Council, Pentridge, Salisbury, Wiltshire SP5 5QX

FACE (UK) (Fédération des Associations de Chasseurs de la CEE), c/o Wood Nash & Winters, 6 Raymond Buildings, Gray's Inn, London, WC1R 5DA

Game Conservancy, Burgate Manor, Fordingbridge, Hampshire SP6 1EF

St Hubert Club, The Apes Hall, Littleport, nr Ely, Cambridgeshire

Glossary

barking	sound of interrogation or alarm made by most species of deer. Usually short and staccato, repeated at intervals.
branchers	young rooks on their nests just before they fly.
brassica	the plant family which includes cabbages, rape, kale, etc.
brenneke	rifled slug for use in a shotgun. The German name derives from its inventor, Wilhelm Brenneke.
buck	male of roe, fallow, muntjac and Chinese water deer.
butt	i. the end of the wooden part of the gun or rifle which is placed against the shoulder when shooting.
	ii. a hide for a Gun, as on a grouse moor.
calf	the young of red and sika deer.
calibre	the internal diameter measurement of a rifle barrel. Calibre may be given in decimal fractions of an inch, e.g. .240ins, or in millimetres, e.g. 7mm.
caudal disc	a creamy or 'off-white' patch seen on the rump of most species of deer. A useful means of identifying departing deer.
centre fire	rifle cartridge in which the primer, which is struck by the firing pin, is in the centre of the base of the round. The term is used to distinguish the cartridge from rim-fire where the primer is located in the rim of the cartridge.
chamber	the portion of a rifle barrel nearest the breech which receives the cartridge when the rifle is loaded.
covert	i. a wood which is regarded as the home of game – usually pheasants.
	ii. a type of feather.
covey	a family party of partridges, grouse, etc.
cranium	the skull.

crepuscular	twilight time.
culling	shooting deer (or other species) to remove a surplus or to reduce the size of a herd.
cull plan	a management plan to control the size of a deer population in the interests of forestry, agriculture and the deer.
cycles	fluctuations of certain animal populations, with highs and lows, occurring at regular or at least recognizable intervals.
doe	female of roe, fallow, muntjac and Chinese water deer.
dorsal stripe	a stripe of longer, coarser and usually darker hair running down the back of some species of deer, commonly red, fallow and sika.
driving	directing the flight of the birds over the Guns some distance away, by means of beaters or walking Guns.
eclipse	the dull, female-like plumage worn by male ducks when re-growing their new flight feathers after moulting.
elevation	the adjustment to a telescopic sight which raises or lowers the point of aim.
fawn	the young of fallow, muntjac and Chinese water deer.
feet/seconds	a measurement of the velocity of a rifle bullet. The bullet travels at so many feet per second.
feral	animals living in the wild and undomesticated in every sense, but descended from enclosed stock. A number of fallow populations in England and Wales are feral.
flanker	men on either side of the beating line – sometimes with flags – whose job is to try to turn towards the Guns any birds which start to break out.
flashes	small, shallow areas of water, sometimes of a temporary nature.
flighting	intercepting one's quarry between two points; as between a feeding and a roosting area.
flush	to force the quarry to rise up and take wing.
foot/pounds	a measurement of the striking energy of a rifle bullet; the force which the bullet exerts on the target.
fraying stock	a tree, sapling or large weed against which a deer rubs its antlers to clean them of velvet or to mark its territory.
gait	the stride or motion of deer
gizzard	a pouch with tough muscular walls into which food passes after swallowing, by certain birds. Grit is retained here to help grind up grains and hard seeds to aid digestion.
grain	measurement of bullet weight in English-speaking countries. For any given calibre, cartridges with a number of different bullet weights are available.
gralloch (Gaelic)	to eviscerate; to remove the entrails and stomach from deer.
gramme	bullet weight in metric-measurement countries.

habitat	natural home or environment (of game).
harbour	place where a stag lies in thick cover.
head	stalker's term for the head and antlers of a stag or buck.
hide	a natural-looking structure, often of cut branches, in which the Gun can hide and from which he can shoot.
hind	female of red and sika deer.
hybridization	cross-mating between two species, for example, between red and sika.
kid	the young of roe deer.
legumes	crops such as peas and beans.
leveret	young hare.
magazine	the receptacle below the bolt in a rifle in which reserve cartridges are held. These are fed into the chamber by the operation of the bolt. Magazines usually hold between three and five cartridges.
magnum	an imprecise term loosely applied to very high-velocity rifles. Opinions differ as to the muzzle velocity at which a rifle becomes a magnum.
melanistic	dark colouration of coat or skin which causes an animal to be darker than normal for its species.
menil	a colour variation of fallow deer which causes the coat to be spotted throughout the year.
muzzle energy	the force or energy of a rifle bullet measured at the muzzle in foot/lbs. Other measurements are now being introduced but most UK riflemen still think in terms of foot/lbs as a measure of energy.
muzzle velocity	the speed or velocity of a rifle bullet measured at the muzzle in feet per second.
myxomatosis	a virus disease affecting rabbits.
off-hand	firing a rifle with the forward hand and arm unsupported. *Not* a recommended method as wounded beasts often result.
palm	the spread or shovel shape of a fallow buck's antlers.
paunched	eviscerated; with the entrails removed.
pedicles	the bony knobs on the skull of stag or buck from which the antlers grow.
peep sight	a metal rear sight for a rifle consisting of a disc with a hole in the middle. Like most metal sights now almost totally supplanted by telescopic sights.
pelage	coat or hair of a deer.
pickers-up	handlers of gundogs trained to retrieve shot and wounded game.
point blank	theoretically, the greatest distance that shot will travel horizontally when a weapon is fired; but it has come to mean very short range at which one is unlikely to miss.

to point	a dog is said to 'point' when it scents game and freezes, pointing towards the quarry.
points	the tines or spikes on a stag or buck's antlers.
pole stage	a plantation at the stage of early thinning.
pollard(ed)	to prune the branches of a tree (such as a willow), leaving a flattish top, fringed with shoots.
porcine	pig-like.
preen	to clean the feathers with the bill.
pricked	struck by shotgun pellets, insufficient to kill instantly.
pull-through	a wad of cleaning or oiling material used in rifle barrels.
Rifle	term applied to a stalker, particularly in the Highlands, to distinguish the sportsman from the professional who accompanies him. Identical to the use of 'Gun' in game shooting.
rifled slug	a single projectile for use in a shotgun. The sides are slotted at an oblique angle to impart spin in the barrel and in subsequent flight (see also brenneke).
roost	a sleeping or resting place, in a tree, on the ground or at sea.
round	cartridge, bullet.
rut	the mating season of the deer.
speculum	a patch of feathers on the wing which are quite different in colour from those near them; most often used to describe the metallic patch on the wing feathers of ducks.
spitzer	American abbreviation of the German *spitzer geschoss* – pointed bullet. A type of bullet with a pointed tip of softer metal designed to expand on impact.
stag	male of red and sika deer.
stalker	a term which can cause some confusion. In Scotland the stalker is a professional who guides the sportsman, the 'Rifle'. In the rest of Great Britain a stalker is anyone who stalks deer to shoot them.
stock	the whole of the wooden part of the gun or rifle.
stock-bedding screws	the screws which hold the barrel and action of rifle to the wooden stock.
stop	someone who is placed in a strategic position in, or on, the edge of a wood where his presence will scare a running pheasant into taking wing over the Guns.
striations	bands, stripes or streaks.
sward	a grassy surface.
trajectory	the path followed by a rifle bullet. Due to the force of gravity this is always a curve. The bullet first rises above the line of sight and then crosses through it and falls below it. In general, the higher the velocity of the cartridge the 'flatter' will be the trajectory.

towered	a bird is said to 'tower' when it soars upwards vertically after being shot. It then plummets to earth and is usually found lying on its back. The towering is caused by the injury which forces the bird to throw its head back in an effort to get more air into its lungs.
trophy	the head and antlers of a stag or buck.
turrets	the knurled knobs on the top and/or side of a telescopic sight used for altering the elevation or windage.
vermiculated	literally, patterned as though by the tracks of worms.
walking-up	shooting – with or without a dog – game that flushes ahead of the walking Gun.
windage	the movement of the point of aim of a telescopic sight to either the right or the left.
zeroing	firing a rifle at a target with the object of correcting the setting of the sights to ensure that the rifle hits the point of aim at the selected range.

Short Bibliography

Game, Wildfowl and Rough Shooting

The Amateur Keeper, Archie Coats, André Deutsch, £4.50

A Coloured Key to the Wildfowl of the World, Peter Scott, Wildfowl Trust, Slimbridge £2.25

Complete Guide to Game Management, ed. C.L. Coles, Barrie & Jenkins, £16.00

The Ferret and Ferreting Guide, Graham Wellstead, David & Charles, £6.50

Gundogs: Training and Field Trials, P.R.A. Moxon, Popular Dogs Publishing, £7.50

Gun Law, G. Sandys-Winch, Shaw & Sons, £1.89

Handbook of Shooting: The Sporting Shotgun, The British Association for Shooting & Conservation, Pelham Books, £5.95

The New Wildfowler in the 1970s, ed. N.N. Sedgwick, P. Whittaker & J. Harrison, Barrie & Jenkins, £3.50[1]

Pigeon Shooting, Archie Coats, Vista Books, Longacre Press, £3.95

The Practical Wildfowler, John Marchington, A. & C. Black, £7.95

The Woodpigeon, R.K. Murton, Collins, £1.25

The Gun Code, British Field Sports Society, 30p

Shooting Sports Handbook, British Shooting Sports Council, 65p

Wildlife: The Law and You, Nature Conservancy Council, 19/20 Belgrave Square, London SW1X 8PY, free leaflet (please enclose sae)

Wild Birds and the Law, Royal Society for the Protection of Birds, The Lodge, Sandy, Beds, free leaflet (please enclose sae)

---

1. At present out of print; second-hand and library copies usually available.

Stalking

Deer Stalking, E. Luxmoore, David & Charles, £8.50

The Fallow Deer, N.G. & D.I. Chapman, Forestry Commission Forest Record 124 (1982), HMSO, £1.35

The Fallow Deer, N.G. & D.I. Chapman, Terence Dalton, £8.95

Field Guide to British Deer, ed. F.J. Taylor Page, Blackwell Scientific Publications, £3.95

High Seats for Deer Management, J.J. Rowe, Forestry Commission leaflet No. 74, HMSO, 80p

Hints on Woodland Stalking, Herbert Fooks & Richard Prior, British Deer Society, £1.00

Red Deer Management, Red Deer Commission, HMSO, £5.00

The Roe Deer, Forestry Commission leaflet No. 99, HMSO, 40p

Roe Deer: Management and Stalking, Richard Prior, Game Conservancy, £1.55

Wild Deer in Britain, Roy A. Harris & K.R. Duff, David & Charles, £4.50

A series of fine booklets published by the British Deer Society:

Fallow Deer, Norma & Donald Chapman, 50p

Muntjac and Chinese Water Deer, Oliver Dansie, Arnold Cooke & Lynn Farrell, £1.75

Sika Deer, M.T. Horwood & E.H. Masters, £1.50

Roe Deer, Peter Delap, 50p

Red Deer, Peter Delap, 50p

Technical Booklets

The following organizations publish informative booklets on different aspects of game and wildfowl conservation, shooting in general, deer stalking and natural history.

British Association for Shooting and Conservation, Marford Mill, Rossett, Wrexham, Clwyd LL12 0HL

British Deer Society, Mill House, Bishopstrow, Warminster, Wiltshire BA12 9HJ

British Field Sports Society, 59 Kennington Road, London SE1 7PZ

Forestry Commission, 231 Corstorphine Road, Edinburgh EH12 7AT

Game Conservancy, Burgate Manor, Fordingbridge, Hampshire SP6 1EF

A list of titles can be obtained by writing to them.

With the exception of the Forestry Commission it is possible to become a member of these organizations, and receive regular reviews and bulletins. Details of subscriptions will be supplied on request.

Magazines

Articles of interest to sportsmen, conservationists and students of wildlife are published in a number of magazines, including: *The Field* (weekly), the *Shooting Times* (weekly) and *Sporting Gun* (monthly).